STRANGE
FOOTPRINTS
ON THE
LAND

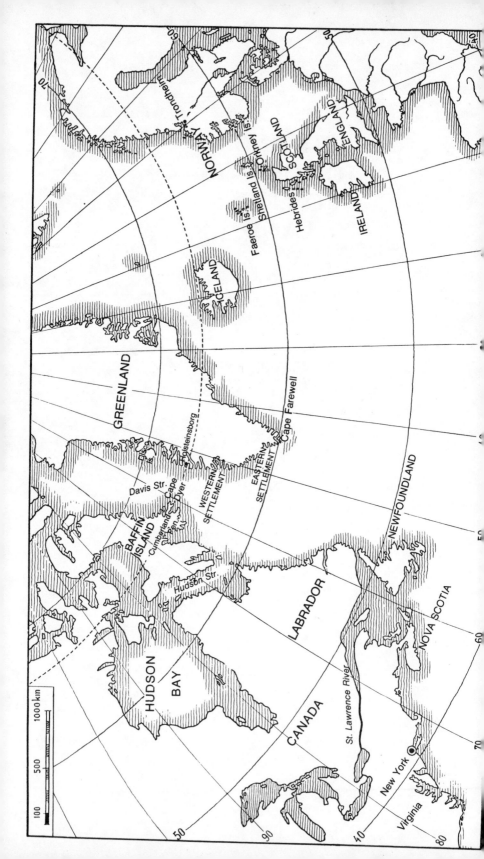

CONSTANCE IRWIN

STRANGE FOOTPRINTS ON THE LAND

Vikings in America

HARPER & ROW, PUBLISHERS

NEW YORK

Cambridge
Hagerstown
Philadelphia
San Francisco

London
Mexico City
São Paulo
Sydney

1817

ACKNOWLEDGMENTS

Grateful acknowledgment is made to the following for permission to reprint material copyrighted or controlled by them:

Gyldendal Norsk Forlag, Oslo, Norway, for the maps on the frontispiece and pages 71 and 108. Reprinted by permission of the publisher from *Vinlandsferdene* by A. W. Brøgger. Copyright © 1937.

Hawthorn Books, Inc., for the map on page 137. Reprinted by permission of Hawthorn Books, Inc. from *Westward from Vinland* by Hjalmar J. Holand, published by Duell, Sloan & Pearce. Copyright © 1940.

W. W. Norton & Company, Inc., for the passages on page 112. Reprinted by permission of the publisher from *The Lost Discovery* by Frederick Pohl, published by W. W. Norton & Company. Copyright © 1952.

Strange Footprints on the Land
Copyright © 1980 by Constance Irwin

FIRST EDITION

Library of Congress Cataloging in Publication Data
Irwin, Constance H   Frick, 1913–
    Strange footprints on the land.

    Bibliography: p.
    Includes index.
    SUMMARY: Examines the detective work historians are performing to solve the mystery of whether Vikings inhabited North America during the five centuries preceding Columbus' arrival.
    1. America—Discovery and exploration—Norse—Juvenile literature. 2. Vikings—Juvenile literature. [1. America—Discovery and exploration—Norse. 2. Vikings] I. Title.
E105.I78 1980   970.01'3   78-19519
ISBN 0-06-022772-9
ISBN 0-06-022773-7 lib. bdg.

For those with
independent minds

Contents

Foreword

Five centuries passed between the day a Norseman first sighted the North American coast and the day Columbus waded ashore on a New World island. To many Americans, probably most, those five centuries are a void. As if nothing happened. In fact, much happened—much that determined the future of our continent. Now modern research is trying to reconstruct that all-but-forgotten past. I propose to look at those years in the light of what specialists have learned.

Not long ago I wrote a novel on the Viking settlement in America. Many who read *Gudrid's Saga* have asked what happened next. Did Norsemen come again? Where did they go? What happened to them? This book goes into those questions and others. It must start at the beginning, with the first sighting of American shores, for those who have not read the novel or who wondered how much to believe. It must also tell you when the evidence is not yet conclusive, show you where it points, and let you decide for yourself.

Though many questions remain unanswered, the picture already emerging is rich and varied. The history of Europeans in America before Columbus, struggling to establish a toehold here or maybe to push on through to reach China, is full of surprises. In courage and perseverance it offers a fitting prelude to the story of two great nations that rose from the soil where Vikings once trod.

Constance Irwin

STRANGE FOOTPRINTS ON THE LAND

I make some coast alluring, some lone isle,
To distant men, who must go there, or die.
                                    Emerson

1
America Discovered

Who discovered America, Columbus or the Vikings? Both. But neither discovered it first. Our first discoverer came from the west on calloused feet instead of sailing out of the sunrise.

For generations tribes trudged through Asia following the wandering beasts that provided food and clothing. At the Bering Strait the clusters of nomads came to land's end. Squatting on their haunches, they stared out across the chill waters. On a clear day they could see a smudge of land on the far horizon and never dreamed they looked from one hemisphere to the other. Up there in the north the Old World and the New reach out to each other. Siberia and Alaska come within fifty miles or so of touching. But people had not yet learned to build boats.

America was discovered by walkers because of climate, that silent molder of history. Over the years the temperature was dropping almost imperceptibly, and glaciers were beginning their slow, relentless growth. Glaciers grow by gathering rain and snowfall and freezing it, locking in more and more of the earth's moisture. In time they lower the level of the seven seas. Just as a sandbar seems to rise from a falling river, so islands rose in shallow Bering Strait. They grew and grew and met and grew until they formed a wide bridge from Siberia to Alaska.

For possibly forty thousand years an earthen bridge linked northern Asia to the Americas—to this empty half-world, this animal world that had never felt the tread of a human foot. One day a skin-clad hunter started walking across that land bridge. He was our true discoverer. Nobody knows when he first set foot on American soil. Nobody knows what he looked like. No one will ever know his name.

It's one of history's poorer jokes that the first name we do know—our first discoverer of written record—is almost such a no-name. It was countless thousands of years later, in A.D. 985, that this man with the clothes and culture of a European sailed along off eastern American shores and stared in amazement. His name and the details of his voyage were recorded and can still be read on parchment puckered and mottled with age. Yet few today have heard his name, and fewer still can pronounce it.

The name is not Christopher Columbus. Nor is it Leif Eriksson. The discoverer so long neglected was Bjarni Herjolfsson.*

Like Leif, he was part of that strange eruption we call the Viking Age, when Norsemen spilled out of Scandinavia in their rakish longships. In the course of three centuries they touched on most of the known world. The Viking wave, washing ever farther west, was foreordained to lap on American shores.

It all began when the great square-sail was perfected and Norsemen could sail, not row, across open seas. At first, near the close of the eighth century, they prowled along English, Scottish, and Irish coasts, raiding and plundering. A few decades later, Norwegian and Danish Vikings were thrusting their grinning dragonhead prows up the great rivers of West-

---

*Pronounced BYAR-ney HER-yulfs-sun. These names are easier than they look if you will remember that in Old Norse (the language of the Vikings) *j* takes the sound of *y*.

ern Europe, the Seine and Rhine, where they shouted demands for *Danegeld*, protection money, in exchange for their promise not to attack. Still later they were plundering along the Mediterranean, Vikings in the narrowest sense of the word: sea raiders.

Not every Viking who left his home, however, was seeking plunder. Many crossed the seas to trade, particularly Swedish Vikings who, from east-facing Sweden, sailed east to Russia. Many more, notably Norwegians and Danes, went looking for homes: not conquest, not even golden booty, but "good and fragrant grass."

Though their reputation abroad was fearsome, in their homeland the Vikings were sheep and dairy farmers. Their cattle required wide fields for grazing. Norway is a long, narrow country with a spine of mountains. When the population expanded, there was little land left unclaimed that was fit for grazing. What's more, when a farmer died his farm passed intact, by law, to his eldest son. His younger sons were left landless. Norway had, however, a thousand miles of coastline facing west, the finest ships, and the great square-sail to carry them far.

Some of these younger sons settled on lonely, windswept, almost treeless Atlantic islands ever farther west from Norway—the Shetlands, the Orkneys, the Hebrides—and began to raise sheep. A thousand years later, some of their descendants are out there still, raising sheep.

Others found the fields of England, Scotland, and Ireland more attractive, though harder come by—sometimes purchased with booty from raids, sometimes taken by sword and battle-ax. Along the northern shores of France, Danes and Norwegians fought a dozen bloody years to conquer the province that still bears their name, Normandy. When the king of France at last yielded the province, he did so on condition that the leader of the Normans, Rollo, kiss the king's foot to symbolize that Rollo was the king's vassal. Rollo would bend a knee to no man. He jerked the king's foot up to his own mouth, causing the king to flop on his backside.

The same fierce spirit of independence provoked another exodus from Norway. It had been a patchwork of many small kingdoms and principalities until Harald Fairhair decided that Norway should be ruled by one king: himself. Years of fighting built to a showdown in 885 in one great, noisy naval battle. "The berserks roared in the midst of battle, the wolfcoats howled and shook the iron." When all was quiet, King Harald Fairhair was sole king. To shore up his throne, he usurped the powers of the chieftains and declared them his vassals. But vassalage was not to their taste. The Fairhair became "The Lousy," and many chieftains sailed away west-over-sea.

Most sailed to an island recently discovered: Iceland. Out in the Atlantic six hundred miles west of Norway, Iceland was far from King Harald's reach. In this almost empty island, land lay free for the taking. There those who refused to bow to Harald Fairhair could build their own nation, to be ruled by laws, not by a king.

This, as time was to show, was the first large step toward America, whose existence was then undreamed of.

The second step followed within a few decades. A Norwegian named Gunnbjorn Ulfsson was sailing off Iceland when his ship was blown off course and far to the west. What he saw out there seemed to be a land and, lying before it, some rocky islets. At this moment the wind must have shifted. At any rate, Gunnbjorn didn't tarry, just ruddered around and headed back to Iceland. He named the islets Gunnbjorn's Skerries, told a few friends, and put the incident out of his mind.

The better part of a century passed before the next step

westward. A belligerent ex-Norwegian named Erik the Red became embroiled in a feud with his Icelandic neighbor, a feud that climaxed in face-to-face combat with ax and sword. Erik won the fight, but he lost to the law. In 981 he stood in court, facing a bench of thirty-six judges on a charge of manslaughter. The judges found him guilty and sentenced him to "the lesser outlawry," a term of three years in exile.

Where to spend three years? He couldn't return to Norway. He and his father, a Norwegian chieftain, had been banished from Norway "because of some killings." Erik readied his ship and confided to a few friends that he planned to sail in search of the land that Gunnbjorn had sighted.

Three years later, in 984, Erik's weather-battered ship nosed again into harbor off western Iceland, and Erik splashed ashore with his news. He had found, he said, a vast, empty land and spent his three years of exile exploring it. It had fields of lush grass bending in the wind, flocks of wild birds spanning the sky, masses of fish, herds of wild animals still unafraid of man, and even driftwood to heat a home. In fact, his new land had everything except people. He named it Greenland. "People," he said, "will be attracted to it if the country has a good name." He invited Icelanders to come out and claim as much land as they wanted. Free. And to bring as many cattle as their ships could carry. There was grass aplenty in Greenland.

His offer came at an opportune time. Iceland, about a century old, had been fully populated for fifty years, when it reached 30,000, and the population was still growing. Though roughly the size of Kentucky, Iceland could offer these dairy farmers only its green fringes. Its center, five sixths of the island, was a wasteland of ice and lava. Erik's vast empty Greenland and its lush grass beckoned.

The following spring, in 985, when Erik set sail again for Greenland, his ship led a proud armada. At castoff each ship was as noisy as Noah's Ark as people shouted farewells, cattle bawled, sheep bleated, and an occasional horse neighed its displeasure. Eight hundred people, the Icelandic Annals tell us, went out that summer to settle Greenland. This was the earliest expedition of settlers to the New World ever recorded in history, for Greenland lies in the New World.

Late that same summer a merchant ship ground ashore at Eyrar on Iceland's southern coast. Bjarni Herjolfsson had come home. Bjarni was a merchant captain, a trader. He and other bold Norse mariners are sometimes called Vikings because they lived and sailed in the Viking Age and for them, as for their cutthroat cousins, the sea was the highway to adventure and wealth.

Even as a boy Bjarni had hankered to follow the sea, and he worked his way up until he owned his own ship. A beauty she was, long and low, her lines running level until they swept up to the pointed prow and stern. In fact, his *knorr* resembled the sleeker longships but was somewhat wider, deeper, sturdier, and therefore more seaworthy: the work-horse of the fleet. Freighters of our day would dwarf her. If we could lay Bjarni's ship on a modern football field, parallel to the yard lines, her swelling waist would extend from the goal to the five-yard line. The tip of that soaring prow would stand above the sideline, and her stern might reach to the nearer hash mark. Here on dry land we can see that from keel to gunwale she is less than a man's height, and underway much of her hull would be submerged. Her prow may have borne the leering wooden head of a dragon to ward off invisible evils, or it may not, as the skipper wished. The thick mast rose to the height of a four-story building and carried one huge sail, which may have been striped in bright colors or merely drab homespun crisscrossed with leather for strength. We can see the crew sitting aboard on wooden benches, ready to man the oars if need be. When one of them stands, all of him from the thighs up becomes visible, for the hull rises only thirty inches above the deck. Overhead is nothing but sky. On a raised platform astern stands Bjarni, manning the stick tiller that controls the rudder, an enormous oar attached to the right (or steerboard, whence our word starboard) side near the stern.

Bjarni had come home to spend the winter with his father. Like other merchant captains, young Bjarni spent alternate winters in some foreign port and at home. Having passed the previous winter in Norway, he was eager to see his father again.

His father, however, wasn't there. Herjolf had sold his farm and gone off to Greenland that spring with Erik the Red.

The news jolted Bjarni, and he refused to unload his cargo. Greenland? He'd never heard of it, though visiting foreign lands was his life. This was a chilly homecoming. Bjarni probably wondered why his father hadn't waited for him. The fact was that if Herjolf had waited he would have missed the big land grab.

Bjarni must surely have asked, "Where in Greenland did my father go?" It's unlikely that anyone in Iceland could have told him. A few of those ships returned before they reached Greenland, beaten back by a terrible storm that drove waves toward them "like mountain ranges." The other ships, friends assumed, went on. *If* they reached Greenland, the settlers had doubtless been busy choosing their land and building long, low houses and thick-walled cow barns of sod and stone, scything grass for winter fodder, gathering wood to heat their homes, and finding the best spots for fishing and hunting so their families could eat. No time to sail back across an ocean to tell their friends they had made it.

The crew asked Bjarni what he proposed to do. He told them he intended to hold to his custom and enjoy the winter in his father's home. "I'll steer for Greenland if you're willing to come with me."

They all said they'd do what he thought best.

"People will call us fools," Bjarni warned. "Not one of us ever has entered the Greenland Sea."

It wasn't as if Bjarni could consult a map or sea chart and let the compass guide him to Greenland. Norsemen in Bjarni's time had no maps, only word-of-mouth sailing directions. Nor could he follow a compass west. Vikings sailed without compasses, which were more than a century in the future. The astrolabe, too, which helped Columbus measure the height of sun and star and learn his latitude on the ocean, was unknown in the north until the fourteenth century, when a priest arrived in Norway with one, causing quite a stir.

The lack of such devices never deterred the Norsemen. They learned to make do with what they had: the North Star and the sun, weather permitting, and often a soaring mountain behind and another far ahead to watch for. Usually they reached their chosen destinations. It's not surprising that Bjarni sailed out into the Greenland Sea.

What *is* surprising is that today we can read the account of his voyage in that rude age and learn how, en route to Greenland, he happened upon the mainland of North America.

We can read it in the very words a medieval scribe copied onto fresh parchment long before Columbus was born. They may or may not be the same homely phrases that Bjarni's contemporaries heard it told in as they gathered around the central hearth in Greenland's sod-and-stone houses in 985, the words their children and grandchildren heard and kept alive through generations until parchment and pen reached Greenland. The words may differ somewhat, but the gist is believed to be the same. This is how Bjarni Herjolfsson discovered America, as recorded in that time-yellowed hand-written document we call the Greenlanders' Saga:

> Nevertheless they put out the moment they were ready and sailed for three days before the land was hidden by the water. Then the fair wind failed and northerly winds and fog came on, so they had no idea which way they were going. These conditions lasted many days. Eventually they saw the sun again and could determine the quarters of the heavens.
> They hoisted sail and sailed all that day before sighting land.

In these few words the Greenlanders' Saga reports the discovery of North America. "They hoisted sail and sailed all that day before sighting land." No shouts of "Eureka!"—only the bald statement of fact. This is a typical saga passage, straightforward and terse.

Listeners in Greenland could fill the gaps from their own experience, but readers today cannot. We need to look again at those few packed lines, this time through the eyes of Greenlanders.

When the speaker said "the land was hidden by the water," his listeners remembered how the white peaks of Iceland had sparkled as they fell away behind, how they shriveled, grayed, and seemed at last to sink down into the sea. Bjarni could no longer steer by the peaks at his back and know the prow was pointing toward Greenland. Any visible landmark helps when you have no compass. Now the ship was alone on a wide, flat, empty ocean.

Later, when "the fair wind failed," they understood that

the wind had dropped, the sail hung limp, and the ship rocked idly, becalmed. Going nowhere. Her one large square-sail was her only means of propulsion except for some oars. When a ship moves at the will of the wind the crew learns patience. But presently the wind came up. "Northerly winds . . ."

No harm in the fact that the wind began to blow out of the north when Bjarni wanted to sail to westward. The crew would swing the sail around, and the ship could make good speed on a crosswind. Listeners in Greenland could close their eyes and see it. The great sail bellying as the ship scudded west, low in the sea from the weight of her cargo. The gunwale, the top edge of the side, so close to the water a man could reach out and almost dabble his fingers in the ocean. The tall prow and sternpost dipping over and righting themselves. No harm in a north wind as long as it didn't rise too much.

But it did.

"Northerly winds and fog came on, so they had no idea which way they were going." To us this might sound as if Bjarni was simply inept—a stupid captain. The fact is, he showed amazing skill finding his way, as we shall presently see.

Some modern geographers and many seafarers believe that Bjarni encountered a "northeaster," a strong storm wind or gale from the northeast that roars down the North Atlantic for days. It's sometimes called a "nine-day wind" and has been known to blow for ten. What would have happened if Bjarni's ship lay in the path of such a wind?

Though the ship was rolling and blown scud stung his eyes, Bjarni would have squinted to windward and checked the rigging to see that the sail wouldn't tear away, then tried to make headway as long as he dared. But the wind continued to rise, driving larger and larger waves before it.

When the ship bathed one side in the ocean and men grabbed at whatever they could reach to avoid being swept off into the sea, Bjarni knew he had to shorten sail. When he looked out and saw long rollers marching down, rollers that could swamp the open ship, he knew it was time to rudder around and take the wind on his tail. Now he must have been scudding southwest.

Again, no harm. Sooner or later he'd have to make southing to reach the southern tip of Greenland. It was just that he'd hoped to hold west until he sighted Greenland's mountains and then alter course when he knew where he was.

The time must have come when Bjarni gave up all thought of making headway. Survival became his sole purpose. At that moment, as captains of sailing craft have done through the ages, he would have turned the ship's prow into the wind, lowered the sail, and cast out the sea anchor. And still the ship would have scudded southwest, driven backward by wind and waves, dragging her anchor through the heaving seas.

"These conditions lasted many days." How many? Afterward, who could remember? During a northeaster all hands would have been too busy bailing or tending the ship or repairing wind-damaged gear to stop and whittle another notch in the day stick. More important to bail as wave after wave lashed over in a curving wall and gushed foaming along the deck. Sometimes bailing went on for days. These ships had no scuppers: that is, no holes in the sides to drain water back into the sea. No pumps, either. Bailing was done by hand, using buckets and whatever the crew could find. Everyone bailed, standing on the slippery, lurching deck with a mere thirty inches of hull rising above it to keep them out of the sea.

Then fog. Fog closing in. The sea growing smaller. Eerie silence after the din of the storm when the wind howled, the ship groaned, and everything rattled and banged. Now silence, and fog rolling nearer until ship and crew were wrapped in its ghostly tendrils. The ship was drifting as if pushed by invisible hands. Not by the wind's fist now but by some unknown current. Drifting in which direction? Again, there was no compass to consult. The fog tickled and smothered and blinded. Men coughed. Which direction, indeed?

At last one morning the fog lifted, and there in its glory hung a pale sun. They "could determine the quarters of the heavens"—north, south, east, west. They did more than just look at the sun. Every Greenlander understood that. At noon when the sun stood highest, Bjarni got out his notched sun stick and held it out so its base lined up with the horizon. By gauging the sun's height against the notches, he could tell roughly how far off course to the south the wind and waves and currents had carried him.

The search for Greenland, he saw, would be long.

It began with the sighting of land. The crew debated among themselves what land this could be. To his mind, Bjarni said, it couldn't be Greenland. The men asked if he wanted to sail to it, and he said, "I intend to sail in close."

Soon they could see that "the country was not mountainous but was covered with woods, and there were low hills."

As Bjarni ghosted in, feeling his way, the crew probably plumbed with lead and line. When the ship lay to offshore with sail lowered and everyone staring, the men may have tried to tell Bjarni this *had* to be Greenland. What else? No other land but Greenland lay beyond Iceland. Yet Bjarni knew from his sun stick that Greenland was many days' sailing farther north.

Not only Bjarni and his crew argued about what land this might be. When later their story was told in Greenland, the hearers argued too. The land Bjarni saw was one no European is known to have ever gazed on before. There wasn't even room for it in the scheme of things. For this was A.D. 985.

In Bjarni's day, Western Europe, just emerging from cultural twilight, had forgotten that ancient Greeks once proved the earth is round. Most men agreed that the earth was a huge flat disk. Seafarers of the North had, from their own observations, reason to doubt this. Mountains behind them not only shriveled; they sank. The polestar moved up or down as they sailed north or south. So they hedged a bit. Their earth was "humped like the back of a turtle." But all agreed there was only one landmass. In the center of the disk, almost filling it, lay the great landmass of Europe, Africa, and Asia: the only landmass, so they believed. Encircling the land was a band of water they called the Great Ocean or Outer Ocean. Its waters were thought to reach to the rim of the world. Beyond it lay nothing. Certainly not two continents that would someday be called America.

This was the state of European knowledge when Bjarni Herjolfsson looked in puzzlement on America. Today as we look at our modern maps there's still a puzzle. No one has ever been able to identify the wooded shore that Bjarni and his men admired as the ship lay to just off it. (Nor, for that matter, the spot where John Cabot landed in 1497 when he gained the title "discoverer of North America" and established England's claim. The West Indies island that Columbus named San Salvador was believed, not many years ago, to have been Cat Island, in the Bahamas. Now Watling Island is preferred; in fact, it's been renamed San Salvador. History changes.)

With Bjarni, however, the problem is wider. Favored sites cover well over a thousand miles—from Massachusetts to Labrador. This though the saga will tell explicitly how many days Bjarni spent at sea between that first sighting and his ultimate harbor. Norse ships sailed, on an average, about 150 miles in a twenty-four-hour day, students of the sagas have calculated from descriptions of voyages of known distance. Why, then, the mystery?

The mystery centers around these tantalizing questions: When Bjarni left that wooded shore, did he turn the ship's stern to shore and head straight out to open sea? Or did he go out only a safe distance and then sail up along the coast, trying to keep land in view as long as it trended in the direction he surmised would lead him to Greenland? When you've answered this to your satisfaction, there's still another. If he followed the coast, does the number of days the saga says he sailed *include coastal sailing*? Or did he *count only days out of sight of land*, as many mariners do today?

Such clues as there are lie only in the Greenlanders' Saga.

Having found land where no land could be, having discovered America, Bjarni still had to find his way to Greenland. Somehow, without map or compass and without even knowing how far west the wind had driven him. He had no instrument to gauge his longitude, not even a watch. (Watches were invented about 1500.) A watch would have told him how much later the sun went down, and from that he might have estimated how far west he had strayed. Lacking a watch, he probably tried in the first days out from Iceland to gauge his speed by dropping a chip of wood off the bow and reciting a verse until the chip cleared the stern. This was some help when the ocean was smooth but none at all in a turbulent sea, and now he was lost.

Bjarni had the sun to guide him by day, if it appeared, and by night the North Star when the sky was clear. Far to the north, as in Iceland, the sun doesn't set until eleven at night in summer and the sky remains milky till dawn, so the star is of limited help; but now he was farther south and summer was ebbing toward autumn. The Viking's "guide star" told him more than direction. By its height above the horizon, which he measured with a notched wooden stick, he could judge how much northing he needed before he reached the latitude of Greenland. These few aids plus his knowledge of the ways of the sea—and his tough little ship and his courage—would have to lead him to Greenland . . . or leave him endlessly seeking it across the face of an empty ocean.

Bjarni was so confident he could find his father that he passed up the chance to spend the winter on this wooded shore. On his way to Greenland he saw more of America. Here are the words of the Greenlanders' Saga from the moment Bjarni upped anchor:

They left the country to port [left] of them and let the sheet turn toward the land. After that they sailed for two days before sighting another land. Again the men asked Bjarni if he thought this was Greenland. He said he thought it was not—any more than the first—"because in Greenland there are said to be huge glaciers."

They soon drew near to this land and could see that it was flat and covered with woods.

At this point the wind dropped. The crew, after talking things over, said it made sense to put ashore here. Bjarni refused. The men claimed they needed both firewood and water, but Bjarni said, "You have no shortage of either." The crew started to grumble. He gave orders to hoist sail [when the wind came up], and they did so. Turning the prow from the land, they sailed out to sea. . . .

Bjarni had now seen two new "lands" and set foot on neither. While the ship lay to off the second land, becalmed when the wind failed, the young crew gathered in groups to fret about waiting—until someone had the happy notion of going ashore. Going ashore how? Probably not by swimming, although most Norsemen could swim like seals. The ship carried an after-boat, about a third as long as the ship. Though the boat was lashed upside down on deck, it could have been lowered with a bit of effort and rowed ashore.

When this was proposed to Bjarni, his gaze must have swept the sky. How soon would the wind come up? If it rose while he and the men were ashore, they would lose precious sailing time. Greenland was still a long way off, and winter was moving closer each day. In winter Icelanders beached their ships. Unlucky the man in an open ship under winter's cruel sky.

The crew grumbled, as crews do today when deprived of shore leave. The responsibility wasn't theirs. Getting ship and crew safely to port before winter was Bjarni's problem.

Sooner or later the mast rocked as a gust of wind caught the ship. Bjarni shouted, "Hoist sail," and the sail banged up and bellied open. This time—and maybe *only* this time— Bjarni seems to have headed straight to sea. That, he probably told himself, should stop all this talk of going ashore. "Turning the prow from the land, they sailed out to sea for three days before a southwest wind."

In that packed sentence are four more words we should not overlook: "before a southwest wind." Why does a saga that seems so sparing of words bother to mention a southwest wind? We know that a Norse captain could sail on a crosswind; he didn't need the wind at his back.

The saga preserved these words because they are all-important. Norsemen described their routes in terms of wind direction. The route was the opposite of the wind named. To put it another way, a southwest wind blows toward the northeast. "They sailed before a southwest wind" is the Viking way of saying that Bjarni sailed northeast.

Why did he choose to sail northeast? How, having lost his way in storm and fog, did he know?

He knew because a certain notch in his wooden stick told him he was still too far south. He knew because a sixth sense he had developed during his years at sea told him he was also too far west. So Greenland must lie to his northeast.

Now, after sailing northeast for three more days, Bjarni sighted a third land. "This one was high and mountainous, topped with a *jökull,*" which can be translated as either ice or a glacier.

Again the crew asked Bjarni if he wanted to put ashore. "No," said Bjarni, "to me this land looks worthless."

So, without even lowering their sail, "they held on along the coast until they saw that this was an island." Once more they put the land astern and held out to sea before the same southwest following wind.

Bjarni had now seen three new "lands" and set foot on none of them. Three chances, and he blew them all. When is a discoverer not a discoverer? Is a footprint on shore the only valid measure of discovery? We could argue that endlessly to no purpose. Bjarni Herjolfsson remains the cornerstone of Viking endeavors in North America.

He shrugged off the third land as worthless. Yet, says the saga, "they held on along the coast." Why bother?

The obvious reason is the comfort the sight of land would give. Even a poor haven in winter is better than the cold gray northern ocean with nothing over your head but the sky. He might have had another reason too, strictly my guess. While his ship was being overhauled and provisioned in Iceland he tried to learn all he could about Greenland. Greenland was a puzzle to Icelanders. Lying out there in the Outer Ocean, it didn't fit in their world picture. Unlike Iceland, Greenland was huge, as Erik the Red had learned. (In fact, it's subcontinental, the world's largest island, Australia being a continent.) Could there be a huge land in the Great Ocean? No, said the wise ones, there is only one landmass. Greenland must be attached to Norway—or maybe to Russia. Surely a long arm of land reaches over from Europe and passes north of Iceland somewhere up in the frozen sea. Greenland, they decided, dangles in the ocean like a giant hand, but it must be attached to Europe.

Bjarni may have heard this in Iceland and hoped his worthless third land was attached to Greenland, just as Greenland was presumably attached to Europe. If so, all he need do was follow the coast. But when the land vanished this hope went with it. "They held on along the coast until they saw that this was an island."

Actually, his third land may or may not have been an island. Bjarni, in a hurry, would not have taken time to sail around it. An airplane pilot at 30,000 feet can often identify an island. A man aboard ship, particularly a Norse ship that rises only a few feet above the waves, is in poor position to judge whether a coastline has plunged into the ocean or merely veered out of sight, even if one of the crew climbs the mast for a better view.

Anyhow, this land didn't seem to link with Greenland, so why pursue it? Here was Bjarni, then, sailing northeast again across strange waters, still looking for Greenland. The saga continues:

Soon the wind freshened, and Bjarni ordered the men to shorten sail and not press on at a speed neither ship nor rigging could bear.

Now they sailed on for four days more and sighted a fourth land. The men asked Bjarni if he thought this would be Greenland or not. "This tallies most closely with what I was told about Greenland," Bjarni answered, "and here we'll make for the land." And so they did.

It was dusk when they landed on a ness and saw a boat drawn up there. On this cape lived Herjolf, Bjarni's father, who had given the promontory its name, Herjolfsness. Bjarni now went to his father's, gave up voyaging, and stayed with his father while Herjolf lived and continued to live there after his father's death.

This incident so annoyed some nineteenth-century critics that they wanted to throw out the whole saga—throw out the baby with the bath water. Bjarni landed right at his father's doorstep. And he didn't even know where his father lived.

There's really nothing odd about this. The saga in its cryptic way merely omits details. Look at it this way. This is how Vikings found their way across trackless ocean.

Before Bjarni left Iceland, he asked and was given directions to Greenland—oral directions. Point your prow due west, he was told. Hold west until you see the mountains of Greenland. Then turn south. You won't find settlers along the east coast. It's a frozen wasteland for hundreds of miles. Erik the Red told Icelanders to sail around Greenland's southern tip. He told them the good land lies beyond it, on the west coast. That's where you'll find the settlers. But above all, don't miss that southern tip.

Almost certainly Bjarni notched it on his stick—notched the height at which the North Star would stand when he reached the latitude of Greenland's southern tip.

If, after his weeks of wandering, he approached Greenland from the southwest, as the saga implies, he had one target. When he held up the stick and the North Star stood at the height of the notch, he should see the mountains of Greenland. If not, he'd better turn and sail due east, always looking, always keeping the polestar at the height of the notch. Guess who lived near the southern tip of Greenland. Bjarni's father, Herjolf. This is no mere happy fancy. Herjolf had chosen a cape along the coast and named it Herjolfsness. Archaeologists digging in the twentieth century have identified Herjolf's estate at the first good harbor west of Greenland's southern tip. Herjolf probably chose it as a trading base for Bjarni. There archaeologists uncovered the ruins of a home almost a thousand years old.

But what if Bjarni didn't approach from the southwest? What if, as some believe, he sailed in from the west? Then, after sighting those massive mountains blanketed under a mile-thick glacier, and after closing with Greenland, he may have spent frustrating days following the coast as it led him southeast. He would have sailed as close to the rocky shore as he dared, always looking for homes. Looking for someone who could tell him where to find his father. But the coast was barren and empty. Greenlanders didn't live on the coast. They sailed up the fjords and built their homes inland, away from attack and the violence of the ocean. Only one man built on the coast—Bjarni's father. Archaeologists have established this fact, too, in the twentieth century.

Greenlanders who listened to Bjarni's story already knew this. Why bother to explain?

It's uncanny that almost a thousand years later, after people had all but forgotten his name, we can read why Bjarni Herjolfsson was sailing in these uncharted waters and how he first sighted our continent. And again today, as it did to those Greenlanders gathered around the fire in their smelly, dark, sod-and-stone houses in 985, to many it comes as news.

This is the strangest fact of all, a mystery worth exploring.

2
History Changes

Why has Bjarni Herjolfsson been neglected? To understand that, we must take a moment to look at this changing world. We accept the fact that as specialists expand their knowledge many things change: automobiles, planes, weaponry, our view of the universe, our concept of humankind's beginnings. We ourselves change as we learn. Even the record of history changes. Pages of the past are filled or revised or possibly deleted. But sometimes it takes a while for newly acquired knowledge to filter down to the schools.

At the dawn of the twentieth century, students were taught that Columbus discovered America. Our first discoverer, he was called, because people assumed that Indians had lived here always, created and procreating in splendid isolation.

A few decades later, students were told that Leif Eriksson came here before Columbus. Leif, they were taught, arrived quite by accident when his ship was blown here from Norway by storms. Once here, he looked about briefly and sailed away. After that, so the fiction continues, nothing much happened for almost five hundred years—until Columbus came—and by that time Leif's Vinland was long forgotten.

Very little of this is true. Yet millions of Americans hold

it as fact. Worse, many children are still learning it today. As they pass through school and depart, they may never learn that Norsemen came to America more often, stayed longer, and saw far more than once was believed. And the Norsemen *tried.* On the success or failure of their efforts hinged the future—your life and mine, our culture, our language.

The full story of their early endeavors in North America will probably never be known. Yet it's still unfolding. Knowledge is constantly expanding, being confirmed or rejected. As scholars learn, the record of history changes.

It changes as archaeologists, digging where vanished people once lived, peel back the layers of earth and reveal its buried secrets. It changes when an ancient book or letter or map comes to light again in some dusty corner. Sometimes a book, its pages browning with time and riddled with wormholes, can tell us things all but forgotten.

This occurred in the case of the Vikings. It happened to Bjarni Herjolfsson. Take the story of just one book.

More than three hundred years ago a huge book, all of it written by hand on parchment, belonged to a farmer who lived on Flatey (Flat Island) in western Iceland. Whether or not anyone in the family could read, which is doubtful, this manuscript wasn't read much: it was too precious to handle. When a scribe bent over a sheet of parchment by the light of a candle and wrote each word with a quill pen, copies were few. This book had been in the family for generations, preserved as an heirloom, protected, almost hidden.

One day a bishop came to call. A bishop was the nearest thing to a king in Iceland, and the farmer got out the manuscript to show. Bishop Brynjolf turned the brittle pages and saw that it was a collection of tales and histories from Viking times. Two and a half centuries before, two priests had collected a number of old manuscripts, copied them on fresh parchment, and assembled the copies in this one massive volume. They completed the task by 1387, more than a century before Columbus discovered America. Who could guess how much light this book might throw on the past?

The bishop offered to buy it. Meeting resistance, he upped his offer from silver to "five hundreds of land"—land on island Iceland, where land could scarcely be bought. Still the farmer refused. Bishop Brynjolf was leaving the island dejectedly when the farmer had a change of heart.

The bishop put this *Flateyjarbók,* or Flatey Book, into the hands of a young Icelander named Torfaeus and told him to deliver it to the king of Denmark. The king placed it in the Royal Library in Copenhagen in 1662, where it may be seen today. It was treated as a curiosity, an antique in an antique language. The world at large remained in ignorance of its astonishing information.

Buried among its pages is the only account of Bjarni Herjolfsson's voyage to America. Also the only detailed account of Leif Eriksson's voyage. And of his brother's. In fact, much of the Flatey Book's information on how Vikings found their way to America, and why, and what they did when they got here, can be found in no other written source that has survived to our time.

The loss of Old Norse manuscripts was tremendous. Some were destroyed by fire, a particular hazard through the long centuries when a wood fire blazed on an open hearth under a thatched roof. Some decayed from damp rot in misty Iceland. Some, as they grew old, were taken apart and the precious parchment put to other uses.

Even so, quite a few survived. Casual mention of Vinland appears in many Old Norse works—enough to establish the bare fact that Norsemen had visited the North American continent. The importance of the Flatey Book and another saga of Vinland called *Eiríks Saga Rauða,* Erik the Red's

Saga, is this: They tell us far more than we can ever learn from those brief side references or from the mute artifacts uncovered by archaeologists. The sagas enlarge our understanding and humanize history. To saga writers, history meant people—people doing interesting things—what they did and why and how.

Erik the Red's Saga, too, can be read today in a library in Copenhagen. Two copies lie there, both from the 1300s. These two copies are so alike they must have been copied from a single lost manuscript. One of the copies we owe to a prominent Icelander named Hauk Erlendsson, who died in 1334. Hauk was so eager to preserve this saga that he hired scribes to copy it. His reason: It tells how his ancestors, a man and wife, led three shiploads of Norse men and women to a new land and established a settlement there.

Finally the man who had carried the Flatey Book to Denmark in his youth, Torfaeus, decided in his old age, when he had become a respected scholar, to write an account of the Norse discoveries of the Viking Age. His was not a translation, but a gist of the events related in the Flatey Book and Erik the Red's Saga. In 1705 some educated Europeans learned what seafarers and churchmen of Scandinavian countries had known for seven hundred years—that Vikings reached a large, unknown land around the year 1000.

And still the sagas themselves remained unpublished.

Not till 1837 did the Vinland sagas themselves appear in print. The Old Norse texts were published, though by that time few could read Old Norse, and alongside were Danish and Latin translations by a Danish scholar named Rafn. (Latin was then still the universal language of scholars.) Through all the centuries since the Norse discovery, only a few had ever read these two sagas. Suddenly thousands read them.

A tempest of controversy erupted. America discovered before Columbus? Preposterous. Arguments raged down into the twentieth century, which accounts for the fact that many Americans learned so little about those who preceded Columbus. History changes, yes. But slowly. Slowly, with caution, after endless wrangling among the experts as they probe for the truth.

First, it was hard to accept that any European stepped ashore before Columbus. Details of Columbus' voyage were etched in the mind of every American. Columbus was America's first hero, the very foundation of American tradition.

Secondly, what proof did we have that these sagas were true? The Norse had no word like *history*, from which we can pluck out *story* and know that one is intended as fact, the other as fiction. The Norse word *saga* can mean either. There were historical sagas and fanciful sagas, and the history was often salted with imagination. How much could we believe?

And even if the medieval scribes who copied these sagas thought they were recording facts, how could they know? The Vinland manuscripts that exist today were written more than three hundred years after the events they describe.

These were formidable stumbling blocks to acceptance. Even in the early twentieth century, if the Viking discovery was mentioned, the popular answer was "Well, maybe. Who knows?"

Meanwhile the detective work continued. Historical sleuthing has its own special fascination. Patient scholars examined every word, dissected every phrase. Few of them could dismiss these sagas as fiction. The Norsemen simply knew too much about North America, and they had put it in writing long before anyone dreamed of a New World.

How could Vikings have learned it except by coming?

How else could they have known, for instance, that in the far north the land is mountainous and rocky—"one great slab of rock"? And that farther south there are sandy beaches sloping gently down to the sea?

How else could Norsemen have known that people lived here? When Vikings discovered Iceland, they reported it had no people except a few Irish monks enjoying the solitude. When Erik the Red discovered Greenland it was uninhabited. Yet in North America the Norsemen found people— people they called Skraelings, meaning "savages" or "screechers." People they described as swarthy and short with long, untidy black hair and broad cheekbones. Strange people indeed to the tall, blond, blue-eyed Norsemen. Not so strange, though, as the half-human monsters the authors of the Middle Ages created when they let their fancies run. Those were as weird as our little green men from Mars.

These sagas describe a food some of the Skraelings carried with them as "deer marrow mixed with blood." We recognize it as a form of pemmican, the rations some North American tribes carried along on their hunting trips.

Norsemen, the scholars decided, must have walked on these shores. When they returned to their homes they talked, as travelers have done through the ages. There was time to talk. Winters were long, and by midafternoon it was darkest night. During those long winter evenings, family and friends gathered around the fire in the windowless houses for conversation. Often they listened to tales of the newest land. The next generation listened, too, and tried to remember every detail. Later, when the Heroic Age had ended, their great-great-grandchildren still heard the same stories. The teller had to stick to the facts or the man at his elbow might correct him.

When a hundred years or more had passed, the sagas were at last written down. Why not sooner? Vikings could write. That is, a few knew how to record their thoughts, using their strange, stiff runic alphabet. But what to write on? Runes were chiseled in stone or carved in wood, which is why, to us, they look stiff and angular. And, more important, why runic inscriptions were short. Longer material was spoken from memory. Even the laws of the land were recited. Runes were not written with easy flow on paper because there was no paper.

Paper, a Chinese invention, had not yet made its way into Europe. Europeans outside Scandinavia were writing on parchment, which is the skin of sheep, calves, or goats—scraped, washed, stretched, and rubbed smooth with pumice. (You can see parchment today in the heads of drums and banjos.) The making and use of parchment, however, was still unknown in Iceland. Finally Christian priests brought it in.

When Norsemen had learned to make parchment and quill pens and use the alphabet we know today, they were eager to write—to write down what they knew, especially their beloved sagas. All of those earliest copies are long lost. Before they vanished, however, the two sagas that concern us most had been copied on fresh parchment.

Today those who know the material best are convinced that *basically* these two Vinland sagas are true. Despite occasional errors and flights of fancy, these facts can be accepted as early American history. The Vikings did find their way to the mainland of North America. They came again and again. And they even established a colony here.

With this much settled, an embarrassing question remains. The only Vinland sagas that have come down to us—Erik's Saga and the Flatey Book version—disagree on several important points. How many expeditions did Vikings make to America? Was Leif Eriksson the first to come? *When the sagas themselves disagree, which one can we believe?*

Again we have a rare chance to watch historians mold history.

Late in the nineteenth century, some of the leading scholars decided that Erik's Saga was the acceptable version. It was better written, more "literary." It seemed to be older. After all, didn't Hauk die in 1334, some fifty years before two priests picked up their quills to copy the Flatey Book? And, perhaps most telling, it exists in two copies, and certain entries in official Icelandic records back it up.

Erik's Saga reported that Leif, while sailing home to Greenland from Norway, was beset by storms and driven across the sea until he came to an unknown land far out in the ocean. He named it Vinland.

At last this version made its way into history textbooks. A generation ago Leif became a familiar name on the lips of schoolchildren.

But even while Leif was becoming a household name, younger scholars were having second thoughts. Why, they asked, are there two versions? Isn't the key to the riddle this: One version records the events as they were told long ago in Greenland, the other as told in Iceland.

Suddenly everything fell into place. The large Vinland section of the Flatey Book is entitled *Grænlendinga Saga*. We call it the Greenlanders' Saga. This saga is much concerned with explorations made by the sons of Erik the Red. And why not? Erik the Red had discovered Greenland. Erik was Greenland's ruling chief. Who would know more than Greenlanders about the voyages made by the sons of Erik?

After all, they and their crews lived in Greenland, sailed from Greenland, and returned to Greenland to report to Greenlanders what had happened.

On the other hand, Erik's Saga, despite its confusing name, shows only slight interest in Erik's sons. What Icelanders wanted to hear, and did, were the American adventures of one of their own, an Icelander, Thorfinn Karlsefni, and the settlement he founded.

Most authorities now agree that the Greenlanders' Saga is more likely authentic in its accounts of the voyages of Erik's three sons. And Erik's Saga on Karlsefni. We shall follow this as our guide.

We can expect soon to see the name of Bjarni Herjolfsson in history textbooks. After all, the Greenlanders themselves, whose ancestors heard it from Leif himself, told that Leif Eriksson was not the first Norseman who saw these American shores. The Greenlanders, who ought to know, gave credit for this to Bjarni.

We left Bjarni on his father's doorstep. The sailor was home from the sea, so happy to be on solid ground he vowed never to leave it again. As he warmed his feet at his father's fire he talked. Talked about three new "lands" he had stumbled upon far out in the Great Ocean.

Did Greenlanders, upon hearing the news, hurry down to their ships? Not with winter coming on.

Did they spend the winter laying plans to sail away the following spring, perhaps in a smaller but proud armada like the one that followed Erik the Red to Greenland, and claim America's choicest sites?

3
Leif Eriksson in Vinland

Nobody bothered. Why should they?

These people had left their farms in Iceland that very summer. They had crossed the Greenland Sea, one of the world's stormiest. They had sailed down Greenland's east coast some four hundred miles past the towering white wall of the glacier with black peaks of mountains poking above it, and past the white tongues of glaciers licking seaward. They had rounded Greenland's southern tip and, from the decks of their ships, stared up at rocky cliffs where thousands of seabirds soared and circled. Sail up the fjords, Erik had said. There were many to choose from.

When a ship nosed in, the voyagers found themselves on a wide blue fjord that was dotted with circles where fish surfaced. Many miles farther up the fjord, the mountains fell back and the land opened out into fields of grass. Thick, lush grass for their herds. The green of Greenland.

So here they were, fewer than eight hundred people including women and children. With their own hands they built houses along the fjords. There was not only grass for their cows and sheep. There was food for their tables: milk, cheese, fish—and butter to spread on the fish. (Fish was their substitute for bread; there was no grain to make bread.) More fish dangled on every drying rack, soon to be stored

for winter eating. At different seasons there would be rein-
deer and seals, sometimes a big white bear (not to mention
wolves), and small wild creatures still unafraid of man.
Every Norseman knew how to flight an arrow. Come spring,
there would be birds' eggs and tender dandelion greens.
There was wood enough from the stunted trees and huge
shaggy stacks of driftwood to warm their homes and cook
their meals for years to come.

They stayed there snug (more or less) in their long, low,
windowless houses. They had built enough furniture to replace what they couldn't bring over in the shallow hulls of
their ships. During those winter nights they gathered around
the open fire that crackled in a pit they had dug in the center
of the hard clay floor and had carefully lined and rimmed
with stones. Smoke drifted up and out through a slatted hole
in the roof. Men sat around playing checkers or chess by the
flickering flame of an oil lamp. Or carving cooking pots from
Greenland soapstone, or repairing their hunting and fishing
gear. Women carded wool from the sheep or stood at their
looms weaving cloth for the family's clothing and new sails
for the ships.

While hands were busy, there was time for conversation.
Children curled up on skins near the fire and listened. The
favorite topic was always people. Next to people, it was ships
and the sea—the sea they all knew and loved and feared. The
sea that brought food and driftwood, brought ships with
people and news, and served as a highway to far places.

Sooner or later, everyone in Greenland heard about
Bjarni's wind-belted voyage and his three new lands. No one
did anything about it, though. Greenland had plenty to offer.
Why uproot themselves again?

So no one stirred until the need was felt. That was about
eighteen years later.

Fifteen of those years had passed when the king of Norway, young Olaf Tryggvason, died in a sea battle. The date was September 9, 1000. Soon after that, Norway had a new ruler, an earl. The news could not have reached Greenland before 1001; ships didn't sail there when winter was near because ice clogged the fjords.

When Bjarni Herjolfsson heard who sat on the throne of Norway he took action. Perhaps he had known the new ruler years ago. Whatever his reason, Bjarni decided to entrust his life to the sea again and go visit the earl. With luck and a fair wind he'd reach Norway in two weeks' sailing. The Greenlanders' Saga tells it this way:

> Bjarni Herjolfsson came over from Greenland to visit Earl Erik, who received him well. Bjarni gave an account of his voyage on which he had sighted those lands. People thought he had shown a sad lack of curiosity because he had nothing to report about them. For this he drew some reproach. Bjarni was made an Earl's Man and returned to Greenland the following summer.

Why, Greenlanders probably asked one another. Why is Norway so interested in those lands?

They could think of several reasons. Norway—narrow, mountainous Norway—had more people than its limited grazing land could support. This had been true even before their own forefathers moved from Norway to Iceland. Men of the north had to have milk and cheese. Cows required wide fields of grass. And Norsemen liked elbow room. Several generations of a family might live in the same house, a house that consisted of one large room, but the home had to have space around it. Acres of land they could call their own. Maybe the earl had ambitions to gain more land for Norway. But land beyond Greenland?

Besides, Greenlanders could use those lands themselves.
Such woods as were standing when the settlers had come out
with Erik the Red were fast disappearing. Over the years
they'd been cut down and burned for fuel. Long, bitter winters ate up long woodpiles. Hungry sheep munched young
saplings before they grew more than a few fingers high.
Settlers were still arriving and needed houses, and though
houses were built of sod and stone they had to have wooden
posts and rafters. Yes, Greenlanders could use those wooded
lands.

"There was now much talk of exploration," the saga adds.
"Leif, the son of Erik the Red of Brattahlid, went to see
Bjarni Herjolfsson and bought his ship from him, and hired
a crew of thirty-five."

The saga didn't bother to say—because everyone understood it—that Leif asked Bjarni how to get there. Which
direction to sail to that worthless third land. From there,
which direction to sail to the next, and the next. How high
the guide star should stand in the sky before he changed
course. What landmarks could guide him.

And Bjarni told him. Bjarni, it seems, knew more than
Norwegians had given him credit for. Though he had failed
to venture ashore, he still, some seventeen years later,
remembered the route and the landmarks.

As Leif laid his plans, it occurred to him that another, not
he, should lead the expedition. The man for the job was his
father, Erik the Red. Erik was lucky, and luck was a quality
Vikings greatly admired. It was part of a man, they believed,
something he could inherit and pass along. Luck meant more
than chance good fortune. It meant the ability to attract or
create good fortune, and then know how to use it. The man
who had luck could accomplish much. Erik had it.

Long ago Erik had turned the misfortune of exile into a personal triumph. Banished from Iceland, he had sailed out and found Gunnbjorn's Skerries. Behind them he found Greenland, vast, subcontinental Greenland. Finding Greenland wasn't enough for Erik. He had spent his three years of exile exploring it. He sailed down its long, bleak eastern coast, saw that people couldn't live there, and kept on going. He rounded Greenland's southern tip and sailed up along the west coast for hundreds of miles. Erik did more than skirt it. He sailed deep into fjords, looking for suitable homesites for Norsemen.

Yes, Erik the Red was the man to explore the lands that had lain across Bjarni Herjolfsson's bow. Leif invited his father to lead the expedition.

At first Erik shook his head. He was getting old, he said. A young man can endure the hardships of the sea and feel only pride in his strength. An old man feels the pain.

Leif appealed to his father. We need your luck, Leif said. "You still command more luck than any of your kinsmen."

At last Erik agreed.

When the ship had been tarred and provisioned and was ready to sail, Erik rode down to it. The distance was short, a few hundred yards, but there was the seabag to carry. On the way, his horse stumbled and threw him. Erik injured his leg.

The injury seems not to have been serious, but Vikings, like others in the Middle Ages, were enormously superstitious. A fall from a horse was a bad omen for a journey.

"It's not my destiny," Erik said, "to discover more lands than this one we live in. This is as far as we go together."

He returned to his house, and Leif and his crew of thirty-five went aboard.

The fate of America would probably have been the same

if Erik the Red had led the expedition. But again, it might not. We shall never know. Erik was a man of imagination. And a promoter. He dreamed dreams, then made them come true through hard work, daring, and perseverance. When Leif cast off, however, Erik was standing before his long-house looking down the green slope to the blue waters of Eriksfjord. He was watching still when, far down the fjord, the big sail rounded a bend and vanished.

From this moment, whatever happened would happen without the guiding mind of Erik the Red.

At the mouth of the fjord, Leif and his men awaited a fair wind and then took off, hoping to follow Bjarni's route in reverse. The year was no earlier than 1003 and possibly a few years later.

One authentic record of Leif's venture still exists. Thanks to two priests who painstakingly copied it, to the Flat Island family who preserved it, and to Bishop Brynjolf, we can read that account today.

Leif was not blown across the sea from Norway by accident. The Greenlanders' Saga tells it this way:

They found first the land that Bjarni had found last. They sailed in close to shore and cast anchor, then put off a boat and went ashore. They could see no grass. Inland lay great glaciers, and from these glaciers to the sea the land was one great slab of rock. This country seemed to them worthless. Leif said, "At least we've done better than Bjarni—we've come ashore. Now I'm going to give this country a name and call it Helluland" [meaning Slab-land, or Land of Flat Rocks].

They returned to the ship, sailed out to sea, and found a second land. Again they sailed in close to the land and cast anchor, lowered a boat, and went ashore. This country was flat and wooded, with broad stretches of white sand wherever they went, and sloped gently down to the sea. "This land," Leif said, "will be named for its resources and called Markland" [literally, Forest-land].

They hurried back to their ship as fast as they could and sailed out to sea with a northeast wind.

We pause to wonder. Why did they hurry back to the ship "as fast as they could"? Could it be that the northeast wind had just sprung up? That Leif had encountered few favoring winds off these shores where winds so often blow from the west? That Leif knew he must sail southwest?

They sailed out to sea with a northeast wind and were out two days before catching sight of land. They held in toward this country and came to an island that lay to the north of it. Here they went ashore and looked about them. The weather was fine, and they saw that there was dew on the grass. They happened to touch the dew with their hands, and when they licked their fingers it seemed to them they had never tasted anything so sweet.

Then they went back to their ship and sailed into a sound that lay between the island and the cape jutting out to the north. They steered west past the cape.

Leif has just turned away from the invisible trail Bjarni Herjolfsson blazed across these waters. Bjarni had sailed along off the coast, probably well off it, with land barely in view except when he moved in for a close look. Three times Bjarni left land behind and struck off across open water.

Now Leif, with Helluland and Markland behind him, was turning inland, steering west. Inland into shallow waters:

At ebb tide there were wide shallows, and their ship went aground. From that point it was a long way to look to the ocean. But they were so eager to get ashore they couldn't wait till the tide rose under the ship. They hurried ashore to a place where a river flowed out of a lake.

As soon as the tide had refloated the ship, they took the boat and rowed out to the ship and brought her up the river and into a lake, where they cast anchor. They carried their leather sleeping bags ashore and built themselves booths [turf-and-stone cabins that could be temporarily roofed with awnings or branches]. Later they decided to spend the winter there and built a large house.

There was no lack of salmon in the river or the lake, bigger salmon than they ever had seen. The land was so kind it seemed to them the cattle would need no winter fodder. No frost came all winter, and the grass withered only a little. Day and night were more nearly of equal length there than in Greenland or Iceland. On the shortest day of the year the sun was visible at *eyktarstaðr* and at *dagmálastaðr* [breakfast time].

This is another of those loaded paragraphs with much to digest. We shall come back to it in the next chapter to examine the *eyktarstaðr* comment and other hints it offers on the location of Leif's campsite. First, though, we'll get along with the saga. We are about to learn how Leif chose the name Vinland.

When they had finished their house building, Leif said to his comrades, "I want to divide our company into two groups now and get this country explored. Half of us will stay here at the house while the other half go exploring. But they are to go only so far that they can get back home the same evening. And they must not become separated."

This they did for a time. Leif himself took turns, either going off with the exploring party or staying behind at the house. Leif was tall and strong, impressive in appearance, a shrewd man, in all ways moderate and just.

One evening it turned out that someone was missing. It was Tyrkir, the German. Leif was greatly upset by this because Tyrkir had been with the family a long time and was devoted to Leif when he was a boy. Leif tongue-lashed his men and prepared to go in search of Tyrkir, taking a dozen men with him.

They had gone only a short distance from the house when they saw Tyrkir coming toward them. They greeted him joyously. Leif noticed at once that his old friend was in high spirits. Tyrkir had a prominent forehead, restless eyes, and a small face. He was a short man, spare and insignificant-looking, but very clever with his hands.

"Why are you so late, foster father?" Leif asked. "And how did you get separated from your companions?"

Tyrkir chattered away in German, rolling his eyes and pulling down his face [making as if chewing]. They had no idea what he was talking about. After a time he spoke in Norse.

"I didn't go much farther than the others, but I have real news. I found vines and grapes."

"Is this true, foster father?" asked Leif.

"Of course it's true!" he answered. "I was born where wine and grapes were plentiful."

After sleeping on it through the night, next morning Leif told his shipmates, "Now we have two jobs to do. On alternate days we'll either gather grapes or we'll cut vines and fell trees to make a cargo for my ship."

This they did, and they filled the after-boat with grapes and cut a full cargo of timber for the ship.

A strange cargo, you may be thinking. What did Leif want with vines?

It's sometimes hard for us to remember that people who don't live in a land of plenty must make use of everything they can find. Norsemen had, for instance, no hemp for ropes. Instead, they used strips of walrus hide. Walrus-hide ropes were strong, but killing a walrus meant making a voyage to Norðrsetur, the hunting grounds in northwest Greenland many hundreds of miles north of the settlement. When men of the family sailed to Norðrsetur they were gone all summer, hunting on land and sea. Meanwhile, here were vines that could serve as ropes. A long rope of braided vines might make a good hawser for mooring a ship or towing an after-boat.

Vines were as flexible, too, as withies, those slender twigs or branches that Norsemen used in shipbuilding so the ship would give a little with the pounding of the sea. Almost certainly Leif used withies on his ship's gear. A few years ago a Norse merchant ship built about the same time as Leif's was brought up from the waters of Denmark. A circle of braided willow twigs still dangled from every cleat. When this ship was sailed a thousand years ago, lines must have been fastened to these rings instead of directly to the cleats to prevent chafing. Brooms, too, were made of twigs—the brooms that swept those hard clay floors of Norse houses. Vines would be less likely to break. And doubtless the ingenious Norse could think of other uses.

The saga doesn't say Leif loaded his ship with vines. His

chief cargo was timber. And he filled the after-boat with
grapes.

With grapes? Possibly with sun-dried grapes, which we
call raisins. Even raisins were a rare treat in Greenland.
(Three centuries later when the bishop of Bergen, Norway,
wanted to send a precious gift to the bishop of Greenland,
he sent a cask of raisins.) The saga neglected to mention what
condition Leif's grapes were in when they reached Greenland.

It's also silent on the subject of wine. Perhaps Tyrkir tried
to make wine and failed. Wine making is a special skill.
Tyrkir, though German, had lived most of his adult life in
Iceland and Greenland, where no one made wine because the
ingredients were lacking.

Now back to the saga, for Leif's adventures were not yet
ended.

When spring came, they made the ship ready and sailed
away. "Leif named the country for its products," the saga
states, "and called it *Vínland*" (literally, Wine-land).

They sailed out to sea and had a fair wind until they
sighted Greenland and its glacier-clad mountains. Then
one of the men spoke up and asked Leif, "Why are you
steering so close to the wind?"

"I have my mind on my steering," Leif answered, "but
on something else, too. Do you see anything strange out
there?"

They said they could see nothing unusual.

"I'm not sure," said Leif, "whether I see a ship or a
reef."

Now the men could see it too and said it must be a reef.
But Leif's sight was so much keener that he could make

out men on the reef. "I want to beat up into the wind,"
Leif said, "so we can reach those people and help them if
they need it. But if they're hostile, we and not they will
have command of the situation."

They approached the reef, lowered their sail, dropped
anchor, and put off a second small boat they had brought
along. Tyrkir called to those on the rock, "Who is your
skipper?"

The leader replied that his name was Thorir, a Norwegian by birth. "And what's your name?"

Leif told him.

"Are you a son of Erik the Red of Brattahlid?"

Leif said he was. "I'll take you all on board my ship and
as much of your possessions as the ship can hold."

The offer accepted, they sailed for Eriksfjord and on to
Brattahlid. After the ship was unloaded, Leif invited Thorir
and his wife, Gudrid, and three men to stay with him, and
he found lodgings elsewhere for the others.

"Leif," the saga adds, "rescued fifteen people from the
rock. From then on he was called Leif the Lucky. He had
gained in both wealth and reputation. That winter a serious
illness fell upon Thorir's men, and Thorir himself died and
a large part of his crew. Erik the Red died also that winter."

Thus ends the account of Leif's American adventure. His
father, Erik the Red, had contributed nothing. Except one
thing of vast importance. Greenland. The stepping-stone
between two worlds. Greenland was then and ever after
the starting point, the port of embarkation for every Norse
ship America-bound, the land they left last and returned to
first—if they returned.

4
Where Was Vinland?

"America's greatest mystery." This is the tag someone has hung on Vinland.

Where was Vinland? Scholars and amateurs alike have tackled the problem and offered more than fifty different answers. They have placed Vinland as far south as Virginia and as far north as Ungava Bay, which lies just west of Labrador's spiky northeast tip. No one has yet convinced all others that any of these solutions meet every specification.

The account of Leif's trek to America offers various clues. To examine them all in depth would require a volume, but here are a few to consider as you have a go at the mystery.

Of all the clues, the *eyktarstaðr* comment seemed most promising. "Day and night were more nearly of equal length there than in Greenland or Iceland. On the shortest day of the year the sun was visible at *eyktarstaðr* and *dagmála-staðr.*" Surely the secret is wrapped in this sentence?

Investigators tried to assign a definite clock time to each of the two key words. But were these mealtimes or astronomical points?

Norsemen, as you know, had no clocks. They divided the circle of the horizon into eight parts and set up large stones, called "eykt marks," on high ground at the divisions, transforming the open country around them into a huge sundial. From the sun's position above the stones a Norseman could estimate, roughly, the time of day. Astronomers, taking the terms to mean solar bearings, have wrestled with the quotation and have come up with answers that dotted Leif's cabins along the coast from Norfolk, Virginia, to central Newfoundland. Even the northernmost estimate, though, was not so far north as L'Anse aux Meadows, those ruins from the Viking Age that we'll look into later in this chapter.

Or were *dagmálastaðr* and *eyktarstaðr* mealtimes? The former means literally "day-meal-stead," but we don't know at what hour Greenlanders ate the morning meal. Four-thirty P.M. was the hour of the *eyktarstaðr* meal in western Iceland and, presumably, in Greenland. After Greenlanders were converted to Christianity, 3 P.M. became an important hour. At 3 P.M. Christians were supposed to stop work on Saturdays and days before a Christian holy day. There's reason to doubt, however, that Greenlanders, then in the early stages of conversion from their pagan gods, had adopted this Christian practice before Leif sailed to Vinland.

If we opt for 3 P.M., we place Vinland far north. If 4:30 P.M., we should look for Leif's cabins in Delaware, New Jersey, New York, or southern New England.

What had seemed the best clue is proving the thorniest. It leaves us, in fact, with only one firm conclusion. If the difference in the time of sunset on the year's shortest day was noticeable to men without clocks—so noticeable as to be worth recording in the saga—Vinland must have lain considerably farther south than southern Greenland.

So, with only the vaguest northern limit, we return to the saga for further clues. "No frost came all winter, and the grass withered only a little." These words immediately precede the *eyktarstaðr* comment and have troubled analysts

almost as much. No frost? The likelihood that the climate
then was a few degrees warmer than today would not account for a frost-free winter. Was this mere hyperbole—the
euphoria of wintering in a climate softer than Greenland's?
Or did lucky Leif happen to catch an unusually mild winter?
Or were these lines borrowed from Karlsefni's description of
Hóp, which we shall read later? The trap of the "no frost"
comment is a temptation to slide Vinland too far south.
Before we do, we must check yet another clue.

The saga speaks of salmon: "There was no lack of salmon
in the river or the lake." Salmon, zoologists tell us, lived in
the Atlantic Ocean from Greenland to Long Island Sound.
This was true before pollution, overfishing, and damming
wiped them out in their southern range—Massachusetts,
Rhode Island, Connecticut, and New York. You might suspect that near their southern limit salmon would be few,
scarcely enough to warrant the statement "there was no lack
of salmon." Yet in colonial times the abundance of salmon
in New England helped attract settlers. The Merrimac River
in Massachusetts reputedly became so crowded with salmon
during spring migration that salmon near the banks were
bumped out onto dry land.

Salmon, then, give us a southern limit for Leif's cabins.
They lay no farther south than 41° North latitude. In other
words, we should look for Leif's cabins no farther south than
Long Island.

And then, of course, there were grapes. Or were there? At
the moment this is a large bone of contention.

Wild grapes today grow no farther north along the coast
than 45°. This is the parallel that cuts Nova Scotia in half,
runs just south of New Brunswick, and cuts across central
Maine. But only southern New England has grapes in abundance along the coast.

In the year 1003 the climate is believed to have been a few degrees warmer than today. If we were wafted by time machine back to that era we probably wouldn't notice the difference, but it was enough to affect plant life. Grapes might have grown as far north as southern Newfoundland, though who can say how abundant they were, how large, or—with fewer days of summer sun—how sweet? Most botanists agree that grapes could not have grown as far north as northern Newfoundland, the site of L'Anse aux Meadows.

So, on the matter of grapes, New England scores highest. But New England, some claim, is surely too far south to have been Leif's Vinland. Nova Scotia, some believe, is too far south.

Those who favor a northern site for Leif's cabins point to the fact that Scandinavians enjoy a cold climate. And that Leif, a practical man, would have chosen a site closer to Greenland for fetching and hauling wood. As the clincher, they offer the sailing time. Leif retraced Bjarni Herjolfsson's route; so go back, they say, to the saga account of Bjarni's voyage from the moment he left his first land (Leif's Vinland?) until he sighted the mountains of Greenland. The saga tells the number of days Bjarni sailed. The total sailing time given would not, they say, have permitted Bjarni to cover a distance greater than from Newfoundland to Greenland.

This might be true if you interpret the number of sailing days to cover the entire stretch, including coastal sailing. But on this the two schools of thought divide. The other group holds that Bjarni, lost, would have kept a coast in view as long as it trended in the right direction. When it came to an end, when the last loom of land astern had faded, the count of days began. It ended when another land was sighted ahead in the hazy distance. They ask: If you include the days of coastal sailing in your total *dægr sigling,* days of sailing, how do you account for grapes where no grapes would grow?

How? By trying to prove Leif found no grapes.

The "northern school" offers three different arguments against grapes. Some maintain that the "grapes" must have been some other kind of wild berry that grows farther north— currants, cranberries, cowberries, or such. A few even wonder if the entire incident was invented and Tyrkir the German never existed. And still others say that Leif named the country not Wine-land but Pasture-land.

This third theory needs a bit of explaining. The Old Norse word that appears in the saga is *Vínland*—with an accent— meaning "Wine-land." Without the accent the word means "Pasture-land." There can be no doubt that pastures appealed strongly to Norsemen. Despite their reputation as sailors and warriors, at home they were dairy farmers. That's why Erik chose the name Greenland. And that, say those who deny the existence of grapes, is why Leif chose the name Pasture-land. What was preserved by word of mouth, some believe, tended to remain correct, but once an author picked up a pen anything could happen.

The reasoning goes down hard, for this is the Greenlanders' Saga. Greenlanders never forgot about Vinland. They remembered which name Leif chose. The saga says it was *Vínland*—Wine-land. Moreover, the word *vin*, meaning "pasture," had gone out of use long before the Vinland voyages.

As to whether Leif gathered grapes or currants or cowberries, the northern school has this to say: Norsemen wouldn't have known. Most of them had never seen a grape. To which the southern school replies: But Tyrkir knew. Tyrkir, reared in the vineyards of Germany, would surely have known. And Tyrkir identified them as grapes.

Still seeking clues, we turn again to the saga. Before Leif found grapes, even before he found Vinland, he had come to a second land and walked on its white sands. Then he and his men hurried back to the ship "and sailed out to sea with a northeast wind and were out two days before catching sight of land. They held in toward this country and came to an island that lay to the north of it."

An island north of the land. This clue has excited many a student of the sagas. At first glance there seem to be few such islands along North America's eastern seaboard. Unfortunately for our purpose, there are too many. Islands lie north of Labrador's spiky tip and north of the upreaching finger of Newfoundland. North of Nova Scotia is a large island, Cape Breton Island. There is reason to believe that Cape Cod, that bent arm of Massachusetts, once had its northern fist cut off by water that covered the narrow wrist. If so, there was also an island north of Cape Cod.

In 1960 a Norwegian named Dr. Helge Ingstad was curious enough about all this that he sailed up along the east coast from New England to Labrador, looking for Vinland. Especially, he tells us, he looked where he expected to find it. That was on the long, north-pointing finger of Newfoundland. When he reached the northern tip of Newfoundland, he sailed west into the Strait of Belle Isle and scanned the shore closely.

As he skirted a grassy terrace that ran down to a shallow bay, Épaves Bay, he thought he saw faint lines of shadows on the grass. He went ashore and found slight ridges, only a few inches high, overgrown with grass. Could they be the remains of Norse houses, their sod walls melted down by the rains, the snows, the winds of almost a thousand years?

Summer after summer, Dr. Ingstad and a staff of trained archaeologists, including his wife, dug at this site, called L'Anse aux Meadows. A short distance back from the shore they uncovered what once was a staggered row of houses—enough, they judged, to have housed about 150 persons. In the houses were central hearths and ember pits. When ashes and charred debris from these were carbon-14 tested, the ruins were dated to the Viking Age. Many dates clustered around the year 1000. (These dates would indicate, not the year the wood was burned, but the year the trees began their growth.)

The archaeologists found a stone lamp like those once used in Iceland. They found several iron nails and rivets, fragments of smelted copper, a small whetstone of eleventh-century Scandinavian type, part of a bone needle of the kind used by Nordic women, and a spindle whorl carved from soapstone. Not much? These people, remember, made their own tools and cherished them.

One tool most useful to women was the spindle whorl, which looks like a small doughnut and was very important in spinning wool. This find, above all, delighted the archaeologists. The spindle whorl at L'Anse aux Meadows looked exactly like others found in Greenland and Iceland. It could not have been used by Indians or Eskimos; neither raised sheep or spun wool.

On the other side of a brook that skirts the settlement the archaeologists unearthed a smithy where someone had extracted iron from bog iron, using a technique employed in Iceland and Greenland during the Viking Age but unknown to Indians or Eskimos. This process was discarded by Europeans long before the day of Columbus. Charcoal in the smith's hearth was carbon tested. It, too, dated from the Viking Age.

The ruins at L'Anse aux Meadows are the first ever accepted as authentic remains of a European settlement in America in pre-Columbian times. They are tangible proof that other Europeans came to America before Columbus— a long time before. And stayed awhile.

A few reporters rushed into print with the long-awaited announcement that Leif's Vinland at last had been found. Many readers still accept this without question. But don't be stampeded. Weigh the evidence and decide for yourself.

Except for grapes, L'Anse aux Meadows offers much that fits the saga: "At ebb tide there were wide shallows, and their ship went aground. From that point it was a long way to look to the ocean. . . . They hurried ashore to a place where a river flowed out of a lake. . . . There was no lack of salmon in the river or the lake."

All true of L'Anse aux Meadows, provided we call Black Duck Brook a river and accept Black Duck Pond, its source three miles inland, as the lake, but . . . "As soon as the tide had refloated the ship, they took the boat and rowed out to the ship and brought her up the river and into a lake, where they cast anchor."

The brook at L'Anse aux Meadows is narrow, winding, and studded with large boulders. Ingstad crossed it by jumping from rock to rock to get to the smithy, and the smith long ago probably reached the smithy the same way. If the brook had been much deeper then, the settlement site would have been flooded. Norse ships were tiny compared with our freighters. To modern eyes, Leif's ship was small, maneuverable, and shallow; she didn't require more than about four feet of water. Yet she was his precious link with civilization. It's hard to believe that, even if he could have, he would have risked trying to sail her up this brook to get to Black Duck Pond.

Leif's crew, having cast anchor in a lake, then "carried their leather sleeping bags ashore and built themselves booths." Did they build, as it sounds, on the shore of the lake? The houses at L'Anse aux Meadows are on the bay; the innermost lies less than a hundred yards from the high-tide line. They are not on the shores of Black Duck Pond, which lies about three miles farther inland.

We might also question the route. Bjarni, we noted earlier, sailed consistently northeast. Leif, if he reversed Bjarni's route, would have sailed southwest from Greenland to Helluland, southwest again from Helluland to Markland, and southwest again from Markland to an island north of a third land. You can study the frontispiece map and judge for yourself if this route would have carried him to L'Anse aux Meadows.

Study it too with these lines in mind: when Leif left his second land, Markland, he and his crew "sailed out to sea with a northeast wind and were out two days before catching sight of land." The voyage from Labrador south to Newfoundland across the Strait of Belle Isle at its widest point is less than forty miles—about a seven-hour sail, though it might have taken longer because of the current. Depending on visibility that day, the crew might have been an hour or two out of sight of land—but not two days.

Where were Leif's cabins? Not likely at L'Anse aux Meadows.

In 1971 a carpenter vacationing in Maine was strolling along the wild west bank of Spirit Pond hoping to find arrowheads and other Indian artifacts. Spirit Pond lies near Popham Beach on a pendant of land east of Portland. The pond itself is tidal, and the carpenter noticed that in one spot the bank had washed away and partly exposed a stone. He cleaned dirt and moss from the stone and saw carvings on it. Looking around for other stones, he found, in all, three that bore markings he couldn't read.

The carpenter, an intelligent man with not much formal education, wisely sought professional help. At a museum the strange marks were identified as runes. Runology, however, is a highly specialized study that requires a knowledge not only of runic writing and Nordic languages but also of different dialects, changes in the language, and changes in the runic alphabet.

Even runologists who possessed this knowledge found the Spirit Pond stones a puzzle. Incised in the first stone is a sketchy map of the area showing the pond, a bit of coastline, and several offshore islands. Beneath the map is the word *Hoop,* and beneath that the words *Vinland 1011.* On the right is an arrow. If you match this map with a modern map of the area and turn the stone accordingly, you see that the arrow points south. Words flanking the arrow seemed meaningless. The text on the other stones also appeared to be gibberish.

This is where matters stood when Alf Mongé, who has devoted most of his life to cryptanalysis, identified them as runic cryptograms.

A cryptogram is writing in code or cipher. Sometimes the secret message is skillfully hidden in "plaintext," a statement that makes sense. At other times the cryptographer makes no effort to conceal the fact that his message is encoded. Then what one reads seems a jumble.

Mongé set to work to solve the riddle of the Spirit Pond stones. He reported that they carry a date in code showing they were carved in the twelfth century. What concerns us here, what applies to Leif, appears on the first stone. Following *Vinland: 1011* Mongé sees instructions to sail *two days south.* Could this be an early form of road sign telling someone to sail south two days to reach Vinland?

The root question remains: Are the Spirit Pond stones genuine? Laboratory tests of the carving on the stones were inconclusive. When stones lie buried, the usual weathering doesn't occur. This left the messages themselves, the so-called internal evidence, as the major basis for judgment. Among runologists who have studied these runes, most believe the messages are fakes. But three cryptanalysts, at least, are convinced that the runic messages are genuine. While the experts wrangle, there is no quick answer.

I have mentioned these Spirit Pond stones for one reason. In the nineteenth and early twentieth century it was popular to assume that Vinland lay in New England, possibly on or near Cape Cod. In the last few decades the popular view has placed Vinland much farther north, probably in Newfoundland. Some feel so certain of this that they ridicule those who champion sites farther south. The recent discovery of the Spirit Pond stones, which might or might not prove genuine, demonstrate that we dare not be dogmatic.

Where was Vinland? "America's greatest mystery" might never be solved. Or the answer might come within a few years. The science of archaeology is young, still maturing, still feeling its way. Techniques for finding what time and the earth have hidden, and tests for dating what is found, are constantly improving. The next generation might learn more of our human past than the earth has yielded to the spade through all the years until now.

5

Thorvald Eriksson
Stretches Vinland

Many people have heard of only one son of Erik the Red, the lucky one. Erik had in fact three sons—Leif, Thorvald, and Thorstein—and a married daughter named Freydis. Each, like the father, sailed the Atlantic seeking a distant land someone else had seen first. And each met a different fate.

During that winter after Leif's return, when illness and death swept the settlement, Vinland was not forgotten. Perhaps it was remembered the more after Erik's death. Perhaps Thorvald, the second son, sat thinking about his father—how Erik, like Leif, had sailed to an unexplored land, how Erik kept looking, kept sailing farther, kept searching. Until at last Erik found the green of Greenland—the narrow ribbon of green that lies between the barren shore and the vast glacier that blankets most of Greenland. . . . And what did Leif find? What did Leif know of his much more fruitful Vinland? Only what lay within half a day's walk from his house.

Thorvald spoke out. Vinland, he said, had not been explored widely enough. Leif said to Thorvald, "If you want to, brother, you may go to Vinland. Take my ship. But first I'll need her to fetch the timber Thorir had on the reef."

So Thorvald, with his brother Leif's advice, set about preparing for the voyage and gathered a crew of thirty men.

When Leif returned from the reef, they outfitted the ship and put to sea. The Greenlanders' Saga goes on:

There is no report of their voyage until they reached Leif's cabins in Vinland. There they laid up the ship and settled in for the winter, catching fish for their food.

In the spring Thorvald said they should overhaul the ship. Meanwhile some of the men should take the ship's boat, sail west along the coast, and explore that region during the summer.

They found the country beautiful and well wooded, with woods stretching almost down to the sea and the white sands. There were a great many islands and shallows. They found no traces of man or beast except on one westerly island, where they found a *kornhjálm*. They found no other man-made things. And they turned back and reached Leif's cabins in the autumn.

We can guess what a *kornhjálm* was by dissecting this interesting Old Norse word. *Korn* means "corn" in the broad European sense: that is, almost any kind of grain. *Hjálm* was an early form of the word "helmet," and Viking helmets were cone shaped. What Thorvald's men saw was probably a conical wooden structure filled with grain. Even if it was only a haystack, it was obviously man-made. The sight must have made their flesh creep. Unlike Erik in empty Greenland, here they were not alone. Somewhere around were people, maybe even watching.

Eastern American Indians in the eleventh century grew no plants, but they did gather and store wild grain. Their storehouses might have been similar to one Henry Hudson saw six centuries later. That was "a house well constructed of oak bark and circular in shape, so that it had the appearance of being well built, with an arched roof. It contained a great quantity of maize or Indian corn, and beans of last year's growth."

Hudson's men looked inside. Thorvald's men were no less curious. And now they knew.

The following summer, so the saga continues, Thorvald "sailed the merchant ship eastward and then north along the coast." A gale rose and drove the ship aground on a cape with such force that the keel broke. The saga adds ruefully: "They had to stay there a long time repairing the ship."

Well they might. The keel was the backbone of the ship, the bottom timber, the longest and strongest, running the full length. When a ship was built, the keel was laid first and all the ribs were attached to it. Replacing the keel meant finding a tall, sturdy tree that would yield at least fifty feet of sound, straight timber in a single piece, five inches thick at the narrow end after the bark had been stripped. Trees in the north are slender, but the coast on which Thorvald was shipwrecked gave him such a tree. (In our own time a favorite source of timber for keels has been Maine.)

When the job was finished, Thorvald said, "I'd like us to erect the old keel here on this cape and call it Kjalarness [Keel Cape]." So they heaved the keel upright and mounted it there. The saga continues:

Afterward they sailed away eastward along the coast and into the mouths of fjords they came to. They sailed up to a promontory that jutted into the sea there and was entirely covered with forest. Mooring the ship alongside, they put out the gangway to the shore, and Thorvald and his entire crew went ashore.

"This is a beautiful place," said Thorvald, "and here I would like to make my home."

As they were returning to the ship they noticed three mounds on the sands, in from the headland. When they walked closer they could see that these were three skin boats—with three men under each.

Thorvald divided his forces, and they seized all the men except one, who escaped in his canoe. The other eight they killed.

Why didn't Thorvald slip past and leave the men sleeping under their overturned boats? Who can say, these thousand years later? Perhaps Thorvald wanted no witnesses to the presence of thirty strangers far from reinforcements. Or perhaps he intended only to capture the natives and carry them off before they could spread the word, but the natives fought back, and the urge of the civilized white man to prove himself superior took over. In Greenland, in Iceland, and all across medieval Europe, violence was the way of life. Existence itself was a struggle, and human life was expendable. Particularly these unknown, dark-skinned, odd-looking fellows they called Skraelings. Now American sands were stained with the first native blood ever known to have been drawn by white men.

Thorvald and his men walked back up to the headland and scanned the countryside. Farther up the fjord they could make out a number of lumps. These, they decided, must be human homes.

The saga now tells a strange story of folly. The Norsemen were weary. The excitement of face-to-face combat was over, their energy drained. "Such a weariness came over them," as the saga puts it. The ship was not far away, but the soft warm sands looked wondrously inviting to men from the gravelly beaches of Greenland. The crew and Thorvald lay down and fell asleep.

They were roused by a loud voice crying out these words: "Wake up, Thorvald, and all your men, if you want to live!

Get aboard ship with all your crew and leave this land as fast as you can!"

Countless skin boats were swarming toward them down the fjord.

Thorvald said, "We must put up the war boards along both gunwales and defend ourselves as best we can, but we'll offer little attack." This they did. The Skraelings shot at them for a while and then turned and fled as fast as they could.

Thorvald asked his men if any of them were wounded. They said they were not. "I have a wound in the armpit," he told them. "An arrow flew in between gunwale and shield and struck me under the arm. Here's the shaft, and it will be the death of me.

"I urge you now, make ready as fast as possible to return. But first you'll take me to that headland where I thought I would like to make my home. I seem to have spoken truth when I said I would dwell there awhile. Bury me there, and set crosses at my head and feet, and let it be called Krossaness [Cross Cape] ever after."

And then Thorvald died.

His men did as he asked and then sailed back to Leif's cabins and rejoined the rest of the crew. They reached there too late in the sailing season to begin the voyage back to Greenland; so they stayed there that winter and gathered a cargo for the ship. In the spring they embarked for Greenland and sailed up Eriksfjord to Brattahlid, "where they had news indeed to tell Leif."

Thorvald Eriksson was dead. The logical man to establish a colony in Vinland was dead. His father had shown how it could be done when he led a flotilla of ships to Greenland. Thorvald was a second son in an age when fathers left every-

thing they owned—land, home, cattle—to the eldest son.
Brattahlid now belonged to Leif. Leif was the ruling chief of
Greenland. Leif's son would, in the course of time, succeed
him. Second sons all across the north were restless sons—
homeless, landless, seeking new worlds to conquer, seeking
new homes. Thorvald thought he had found the spot. "This
is a beautiful place, and here I would like to make my home."

The words were only a few hours old when he murdered
eight Skraelings. Eight men who might have become his
neighbors and friends. The land was large enough, fruitful
enough for all—until the old Viking bloodlust broke
through. Now Thorvald lay dead, the first white man known
to have died of an Indian arrow. (It had to be Indian.
Though Eskimos lived farther south then than now, the only
Eskimos who might have been in these parts had not, so far
as is known, learned the use of bow and arrow this early.)

Thorvald had indeed been his father's son, quick with the
sword, but his father's son, too, in courage and enterprise.
We think of him lying forever in Vinland, but this was not
Leif's little Vinland. This was Thorvald Eriksson's Vinland,
a much larger land. Vinland would never again mean only
Leif's one small spot. Thorvald Eriksson had stretched it.

Few students of the saga today agree on the range of
Thorvald's expedition. Some tell us his men must have shut-
tled about in a narrow space on northern waters. Perhaps.
But more likely Thorvald, having criticized Leif for seeing
too little, sailed as far as time permitted. Probably not so far
as his father, but holding his father's example in mind. Erik
the Red had looked at a thousand miles of Greenland coast
and still had taken the trouble to sail into and far up promising fjords. Thorvald's crew described a coast where woods
stretch almost down to the sea and the white sands, and
many islands float among shallows. This combination, as

others, too, have noted, is typical of New England's southern coast and more southerly American waters.

Now the crew was home in Greenland, home without their captain. Home with "news indeed to tell Leif." In due time the news reached the youngest of Erik's three sons. He took action.

Erik's youngest son was Thorstein. Like thousands of others in his birthland, Iceland, he was named for the red-bearded god of thunder, Thor, who had been the pagan Icelanders' favorite god. The saga says of Thorstein: "No man in Greenland was considered as promising as he."

While his brother Thorvald was off in Vinland, Thorstein married Gudrid Thorbjornsdottir, one of the fifteen ship-wrecked people Leif had rescued from the reef. At the time of the rescue she was the wife of the Norwegian captain, Thorir, who died the following winter in the same epidemic that took Erik the Red. Gudrid, the saga reports, was "a most beautiful woman, distinguished in every trait."

Erik's third son left the family home when he married and had to look for land elsewhere. Green pastures were far to seek in Greenland, for the population was growing. All the good land along Eriksfjord had been claimed, and that along other southern fjords, too. So Thorstein and Gudrid left the Eastern Settlement and sailed northwest up the coast some four hundred miles to the vicinity of what is now Godthaab. There they sailed between soaring mountains and entered a fjord. Along the shores of Lysufjord a second settlement was springing up, the Western Settlement. Here Erik's youngest son built his home, and here news of Thorvald's death in Vinland reached him.

Thorstein, hearing the news, announced that he would sail to Vinland and bring back his brother's body.

It was not a Viking custom to bring back the bodies of Norsemen who died on foreign soil. Instead, back in the homeland a memorial stone was erected and the name was inscribed on it in runes. Thorstein, however, like his brothers, had become a Christian. The heathen ways wouldn't do. His brother must have Christian burial and lie in hallowed ground. His mother had built a tiny church, the first in Greenland, and a Christian graveyard encircled it.

Thorstein's wife, Gudrid, decided to go to Vinland with him. In most of Europe during the Middle Ages a woman's opinion didn't carry much weight. Her husband's was the opinion that counted. Across the north, however, women commanded more respect. A Scandinavian woman expressed her views freely, and more often than not her husband heeded. So Gudrid Thorbjornsdottir became the first woman of written record to sail in search of America.

For this mission, which might be dangerous, Thorstein selected a crew of twenty-five, "the biggest and strongest men he could find." They took little cargo, largely weapons, food, and gear.

Probably Thorstein intended to bypass Helluland and Markland. Why bother with them? Exploration wasn't his mission. So he may have followed the old Viking practice of latitude sailing. That is, from Greenland he may have sailed south or southwest, intending to hold that course till he reached the latitude he wanted and then head due west for his brother's beautiful headland, Cross Cape.

Somewhere out on the ocean a storm caught the ship. Then a series of storms. "All summer long they were storm driven over the sea," the Greenlanders' Saga tells in its sparing account, "and they had no notion where they were going." Or where they were.

Erik's Saga adds a few details of these harried months: "A

long time they were tossed about on the ocean and could not hold to the course they intended. They came in sight of Iceland. Another time they saw birds from Ireland."

Thorstein's was not the first Norse ship to wander the sea all summer at the mercy of the weather. Even on the shorter crossing from Iceland to Greenland, sometimes a voyage took only a few days, sometimes it lasted months. And sometimes it ended in shipwreck on the treacherous Greenland coast. In later years a Greenlander with the gruesome name of Corpse-Lodin had as his occupation picking up bodies along the east coast and transporting them to a churchyard.

Thorstein's voyage is more revealing than any series of smooth sailings. Norse *knerrir* (plural; singular: *knorr*) were seaworthy and sturdy, beautiful as a modern yacht, but they sailed nonetheless at the whim of the wind. A skillful helmsman could sail close to the wind by zigging and zagging, but his ship was light and shallow and had little grip on the water. She was designed to ride the crests of waves, not plow through them, and holding course in a heavy blow was often impossible. When seas ran high and gale winds blew, Thorstein must have felt as if he were trying to steer a nutshell on a torrent.

If the birds he saw were truly from Ireland, if the land he glimpsed was Iceland, whose distinctive white peaks are visible a hundred miles at sea, he had to reach a decision. Knowing his whereabouts at last, he could try again for Vinland. Or he could steer instead for Greenland and hope to reach home before winter—before the sail crackled with ice, before men had to beat their arms against their sides to keep from freezing, before the barrels of dwindling food and brackish water were empty. It was a hard decision that bruised his pride.

He almost made it home.

"One week after the beginning of winter," the Greenland-ers' Saga reports, "they reached Lysufjord in Greenland in the Western Settlement." They entered the fjord, it seems, but farther along it must have been clogged with ice. Thor-stein, like his father, had built his home at the inner end of the fjord, and the water road was closed for the winter. So Thorstein trudged about and found lodgings for all his crew at the few scattered farmhouses—but none for himself and his wife. They had slept two nights aboard ship when a black-bearded stranger appeared and invited Thorstein and Gudrid to spend the winter in his home.

Soon a disease broke out among Thorstein's crew, and many of them died. Then Thorstein himself fell ill. Death closed the career of Erik the Red's unlucky son.

Thorstein Eriksson never reached Vinland. Erik's young-est, most promising son was not granted time to fulfill his early promise. Nor to write his name beneath those of his father and brothers on the list of the world's successful ex-plorers. Thorstein's story belongs with the Vinland voyages, however, if only for balance.

Amid the triumphs it reminds us that the sea can be gentle or cruel, man's servant or man's master. That all these Vin-land voyages were undertaken without motor or map or compass or even a deck overhead. That life in the Middle Ages was a fragile thing, and more often than not it was brief.

6
The Viking-Age Settlement in America

It was inevitable that sooner or later someone would conceive the idea of founding a settlement in Vinland. The instigator seems to have been a woman—Gudrid, the widow of Thorstein Eriksson. Gudrid returned to the Eastern Settlement in the spring with her silent shipmates when their bodies were taken there for burial as Thorstein had directed. There Leif, as her next of kin, invited her to live in his home, Brattahlid.

Late that summer a large square-sail hove into view down the fjord. Behind it, bending taut, was another sail. Two foreign merchant ships were approaching. Along the fjord rose shouts and the thud of galloping hoofs as Greenlanders rode to the quay in the hope of buying things Greenland couldn't provide—luxuries from Europe, fine linens, wheat, barley, and malt. These Icelandic merchants had called at Norway. If the cargo was right, Greenlanders could bake up some bread and brew some ale, those rare treats.

Leif invited the crews to be guests at Brattahlid for the winter. This was a northern custom, but two crews at once were a bit much for a one-room hall. Some slept on the benches that lined the walls, many must have slept on the floor all winter, and others probably bunked in the thrall house, the servants' quarters.

Just after Christmas the beautiful Gudrid received a pro-
posal of marriage from the captain of the larger ship. He was
Thorfinn Thorsdarsson, nicknamed Karlsefni, meaning
"stuff of a man." Karlsefni and Gudrid were married, and
the wedding was celebrated by three days of festive eating
and drinking.

During the long winter months that followed, there was,
of course, talk of Vinland. "Gudrid and others," as the
Greenlanders' Saga puts it, "urged Karlsefni to undertake an
expedition." This was to be an expedition of settlement.

Why the idea appealed to Karlsefni, why this wealthy
Icelander from an eminent family would choose to live in a
wilderness, we can only surmise. Karlsefni was of the new
breed of Vikings, a merchant captain who voyaged far. But
plenty of the old breed of Vikings studded his family tree,
including Ragnar Hairybreeks, "greatest of Vikings," and
others who had raided, sacked, and conquered. Some had
carried off slaves from Mediterranean shores. Others of his
forebears had ruled portions of England, Scotland, and Ireland. Karlsefni may have hoped to prove to himself that he
was no less a man than those Vikings of old. He, too, could
sail out and claim a new land. Without drawing his sword
from its scabbard.

This was to be such an expedition as had never before set
sail for Vinland. There would be three ships: Karlsefni's, the
other visiting merchant ship (whose crew also were Icelanders), and one shipload of Greenlanders. Sixty men and five
women crowded into Karlsefni's ship. All together, so Erik's
Saga reports, 160 people took part in the expedition. The
Greenlanders' Saga adds: "They took livestock of all kinds
because they intended to make a permanent settlement if
they could."

The decision to settle in Vinland was, we can be sure, not

reached lightly. They had to weigh the assets of Vinland—the forests and meadows, softer winters, longer summers for growing food—against the distance. A Norseman aboard a dependable ship often thumbed his nose at distance, like an American today with a superhighway under his wheels. But a settlement far from civilization needs help to survive. Merchant ships had to keep coming. Who would send ships to far-off Vinland? Who would send people?

Karlsefni may have decided to gamble that Iceland would help. His native Iceland, not Greenland. Greenland's few people—possibly two or three thousand in all at that moment—were not enough. Greenland's few ships were needed for voyages to Norðrsetur, the northern hunting grounds. There bold hunters bagged not only meat for their tables and blubber for their lamps but also the products that kept the foreign ships coming to Greenland—ivory tusks from the walrus and the long, twisted ivory horn of the narwhal for ivory-hungry Europe.

Iceland, on the other hand, had forty or possibly fifty thousand people by this time—and no more land for grazing. All those second sons growing to manhood were landless. Also, Icelanders, like Greenlanders, had used up most of the woods that were standing when the first settlers came out and now they could grow no more. Wood was the fuel that warmed their homes and cooked their food. And Icelanders needed furs; an island far out in the ocean has no vast supply of wild beasts. Surely Icelanders would come to Vinland for timber and furs? And some might return to stay?

There were Skraelings, too, to consider. But Leif had met no Skraelings. Maybe none lived near his house. "Karlsefni," the Greenlanders' Saga tells, "asked Leif for his house in Vinland. Leif said he would lend it but not give it."

It was spring of the year 1011* or thereabout when the three ships assembled at the mouth of Eriksfjord and waited to run off together before a fair wind. Each was crowded with people and bawling cattle. Yet spirits soared. They were off to settle a new land, and they were the first. Adventures like this were the stuff of sagas. Who knew how long their names might live on in a story? Or how great a nation they might found?

"They sailed first to the Western Settlement and thence to the Bear Isles." Why? The two settlements, Eastern and Western, might more accurately have been called Northern and Southern. Why sail four hundred miles north to the Western Settlement when their destination lay south?

Karlsefni probably wanted to check out Thorstein Eriksson's estate, which now belonged to Gudrid, before he went on. And probably, with all those mouths to feed and all those cattle, irreplaceable in Vinland, he hoped to shorten the stretches of open-sea sailing and reduce the risk of being blown off course. It was not by chance that he found a narrower crossing from Greenland to America. Someone must have told this stranger that if he sailed to the Western Settlement and from there sailed north again for a day or two, then turned and headed due west where the current turns west, he would soon come to another land.

Some think today that he was merely following Leif's

---

*If we accept 1003 as most likely the year that Leif set out to retrace Bjarni's route, and if we add the various time spans indicated in the Greenlanders' Saga, we arrive at this speculative chronology, which takes into consideration the fact that Thorstein Eriksson lived in the Western Settlement and had to be notified of Thorvald's death, outfit a ship, and assemble a crew: 1004, Leif returns to Greenland; 1005, Thorvald sails for Vinland; 1006, Thorvald sends an expedition to explore to the south; 1007, Thorvald is killed while exploring to the north; 1008, Thorvald's crew returns to Eriksfjord; 1009, Thorstein sails for Vinland; 1010, Karlsefni arrives in Greenland; 1011, Karlsefni embarks for Vinland.

route—Leif's, Thorvald's, and Thorstein's. There is not one word in the sagas to support this. On the contrary: Leif retraced Bjarni's route, and Bjarni Herjolfsson, in a hurry, would have had no reason to sail so far north. A better clue lies in Erik's Saga.

Among those aboard the Greenland ship, the saga tells us, were Erik's illegitimate daughter, Freydis; her husband, Thorvard; and an unpopular old pagan called Thorhall the Hunter. This Thorhall the Hunter is described (by no friend) as giant-sized, swarthy, overbearing, cunning, abusive, and always ready to stir up trouble. He was taken along, the saga explains, "because he had wide knowledge of the unsettled regions."

The "unsettled regions" Thorhall the Hunter knew were not Vinland, as we shall see. They might have been familiar old Norðrsetur. Or they might have been, and probably were, that cold, unpeopled land across the waters west of Greenland. We call it Baffin Island, in eastern Canada. The mountains of its east-reaching arm, Cumberland Peninsula, were dimly visible on a clear day from atop high mountains about a day's sail north of the Western Settlement. If anyone knew that wilderness, Thorhall the Hunter would have. It had the richest hunting grounds of the North, richer even than Norðrsetur. He could lead the expedition across.

We will try to follow as the three ships sail across Davis Strait with the mountains of Greenland falling away behind. Their next stop is the Bear Isles. The Bear Isles offer a fixed spot from which to take our bearings, so it's awkward that they're unknown. They were probably those islets off Cumberland Peninsula where polar bears still gather today.

From there they sailed before a north wind [sailed south] and were at sea two days. Then they found land and rowed

ashore in boats. They found there huge slabs of rocks,
many of them eighteen feet wide. There were numerous
arctic foxes there. They gave this country a name and
called it Helluland, Land of Flat Stones.

It may or may not have been the same Helluland as Leif's.
Karlsefni's Helluland was probably the grim northern tip of
Labrador, which has just such slabs of rock and white foxes
and little else.

From Helluland they sailed south and southeast and came
to a wooded country with many animals. They named it
Markland. (It never bothered a Norseman that a name had
been used before.) This might still have been Labrador. If the
ships were sailing far out, keeping the mountains dimly in
view off this wind-whipped coast, Karlsefni may have
thought the land ended when the mountains did. Here the
land dips west at the great Nain Bight, that long, shallow
indentation in the Labrador coast, then swings again east
considerably farther south.

Leaving Markland, the ships "sailed southward along the
coast for long hours and came to a cape. The land lay to
starboard. It was an open, harborless coast with long, sandy
beaches." To Norsemen accustomed to Iceland's black lava
beaches or Greenland's gravelly shores, these golden sands
were marvelous. So they named them Furdustrandir, Marvelous Strands. They named the cape Kjalarness, Keel Cape.

Keel Cape. Does this mean they had found the broken keel
of Thorvald Eriksson's ship? Most students of the sagas
today think not. They believe instead that the ships were
passing Labrador's Porcupine Strand, a forty-mile stretch of
just such sandy beaches, and came to Cape Porcupine. This
peninsula, shaped like the hull of an overturned ship, juts
two miles out into the Atlantic from Porcupine Strand.

Norsemen had given the name Keel Cape to similar formations in the north.

"They held on their way," the saga continues, "until the land was indented by a fjord." The fjord had a strong current, so they called it Straumfjord, meaning "Current Fjord."

If we've followed the triple wake of the ships correctly so far, this Current Fjord was probably the Strait of Belle Isle. As it pours out between Labrador and Newfoundland, both its size and powerful current would have impressed the voyagers.

"Into this fjord they steered their ships." Which way? West along Labrador's southern coast? Or south across the fjord? Almost certainly they crossed the fjord. A glimpse of Labrador's southern coast would have repelled them. Nothing but high, rocky cliffs bare of soil and vegetation. When Jacques Cartier saw it five centuries later, he called it "the land God gave to Cain."

On the other side it's a different picture. If the voyagers crossed the Strait of Belle Isle, their first view of Newfoundland would have been Cape Bauld, the northern tip. Turning west at Cape Bauld and sailing along Newfoundland's northern shore, they would have found the coastline carved into bays, many bays large and small, and dotted with islands.

"They held on into the fjord and called it Straumfjord. Here they carried their goods off the ships and prepared to stay."

"Here," says the saga elliptically. But where was "here"? It might have been any promising site along this shore. Except that now we get help from archaeologists.

Five miles west of Cape Bauld, on Épaves Bay, near the tiny fishing village of L'Anse aux Meadows, Dr. Helge Ingstad found the remains of the settlement described on pages 48–52. Years of digging, you recall, turned up artifacts that identified the ruins as Norse. Carbon-14 tests dated them as of these early decades of Norse exploration.

Nothing here bore the name of Karlsefni, nothing labeled the settlement his, nothing linked it beyond doubt to any one group. If ever a Norseman sat here carving a runic message, it has vanished. There is no proof, nor likely ever will be, that L'Anse aux Meadows was Karlsefni's Straumfjord.

Still, there are hints. The most emphatic is that strange little doughnut-shaped gadget carved from soapstone, the spindle whorl. A Norse woman couldn't work her wool without it. It implies the presence of women and sheep. Karlsefni's expedition had both. Almost a thousand years ago a woman sat outside at her woolwork (anything to get out of those windowless houses) and lost her spindle whorl in the tall grass. Over the centuries Indians and Eskimos came and went, picking up everything of value. To people who had no freshly shorn wool, however, and no sheep, a spindle whorl is useless.

There's also the matter of numbers. Archaeologists have estimated that the settlement at L'Anse aux Meadows housed, in that long-ago day, about 150 persons. The saga tells us that 160 people sailed with Karlsefni. His was the only known expedition so large. It seems likely, though unprovable, that the settlers at L'Anse aux Meadows came there with Thorfinn Karlsefni.

This brings us to a major contradiction between the two sagas.

We've followed Karlsefni's expedition from Greenland to Straumfjord through details recorded in Erik's Saga, the account as reported in Iceland. The Greenlanders' Saga, on the other hand, tells only this from the moment of departure. "They put to sea and arrived safe and sound at Leif's cabins."

Which to believe? Did Leif's, Thorvald's, and Karlsefni's expeditions all headquarter at the same place? Could this be, when Leif, if he followed Bjarni's route, sailed consistently southwest? When Leif sailed up a river and apparently built on the shore of a lake, and the houses at L'Anse aux Meadows lie near the bay? Were scribes in Iceland silent about Leif's cabins out of national pride? And because their skimpy account of Leif's voyage failed to mention cabins?

Many think so. Yet scribes in Iceland were not too proud to admit that master mariner Karlsefni, an Icelandic hero, searched for and could not find Leif's Vinland. Icelandic scribes tell us that a year later Karlsefni and his people debated whether to go north or south to find Leif's Vinland, which could only mean Leif's cabins. A year after that, Karlsefni was searching again for Vinland.

If the Greenland version erred in placing Karlsefni at Leif's cabins, how could it happen? Probably like this. Greenlanders all through the years were interested in what Erik and his sons accomplished. Karlsefni, however, was an Icelander, and two of the three ships in his expedition came from Iceland, their crews likewise. Greenlanders cared little about this expedition, and in time they simply forgot details. They may have borrowed a line from the saga that describes Thorvald Eriksson's voyage outward bound: "They put to sea, and there are no reports of their voyage until they reached Leif's cabins in Vinland."

Putting conjecture aside, let's get on with the story.

Summer gave way to autumn, and Karlsefni's wife, Gudrid, gave birth to a son, the first white child of record born in America—about 576 years before Virginia Dare. Karlsefni and Gudrid chose a less musical name. They called their son Snorri.

All too soon autumn faded into winter—the first winter in America of the first Europeans who came here to make their home. They expected it to be mild and possibly frostless. "They stayed there that winter, and a hard one it was. They had made no provisions for it, and now food ran short and the hunting and fishing failed."

Rather than starve, they moved out to an island where they hoped the fishing would be better or something might drift ashore. Days later something did—a whale. A whale at sea was a terror. Rising huge and wet from the ocean, sometimes longer than the ship, it had to be frightened away by shouting and banging and dropping empty barrels into the sea. But a whale on land was a supermarket come to their door.

In the spring the colonists moved back to Straumfjord. Spring brought a more varied menu, including returning game. The men hunted game on the mainland, gathered eggs from the island, and caught fish from the sea. Even so, Straumfjord had lost its charm.

This was the hour of decision. The Icelandic saga describes it:

Now they discussed their expedition and laid plans. Thorhall the Hunter wanted to go north past Marvelous Strands and Keel Cape and search for Vinland there. Karlsefni, though, wanted to sail south along the coast, and east of it, for he believed the country would improve the farther south they went. And it seemed to him advisable to explore in both directions.

This rather sounds as if Karlsefni yielded gracefully to the inevitable in letting the Huntsman go his own way. Norsemen prided themselves on their independence, particularly

Thorhall the Hunter. Nine men decided to go with Thorhall.
They probably used one of the after-boats, because the 150
who remained with Karlsefni were too many to have
crowded into two ships along with goods and cattle.

First the Huntsman overhauled and stocked his vessel.
One day, as he was carrying water to it, he stopped and
drank from the bucket and recited this verse:

> Warriors promised when I came here
> I would quench my thirst with wine,
> Best of drinks a man can dream of.
> Curse this land they called divine!
> Now behold this helmet wearer—
> Stooping at the spring he sips.
> Here I lug a water bucket;
> Wine has not yet touched my lips.

The Huntsman never doubted that Vinland meant wine.

When the little group put to sea, Karlsefni in a gesture of
friendship took an after-boat and rowed alongside them out
past the islands. Before Thorhall ordered his men to hoist
sail, the Huntsman recited this verse:

> Sailors, let us skim the main
> To Greenland and our friends again,
> While drudges who can praise these lands
> Go boil a whale on Marvel Strands.

Then he sailed away, leaving Karlsefni to fume and wonder.

Thorhall, it seems, was only having a little joke. The saga,
drawing on later information, tells us that Thorhall and his
crew of nine sailed north past Marvelous Strands and Keel

Cape and "wanted to beat to westward." North of Keel Cape lies Hamilton Inlet, a promising bay, and Thorhall apparently hoped to sail in and look for Leif's cabins. "But gales out of the west drove them across to Ireland. There they were brutally beaten and thrown into slavery. And there Thorhall died, so traders have reported."

Thorhall the Hunter was dead. Back at Straumfjord, however, those who remained had no way of knowing his fate. They went on with their preparations to sail south, believing with Karlsefni that "the country would improve the farther south they went."

The task of finding the site for their settlement still lay ahead. The shiploads of immigrants sailed south. This much we know from Erik's Saga. We know too that "they sailed for a long time." This site had to be chosen with more care than Straumfjord: It was more important. It was more important even than Leif's Vinland, for this more southerly location was to be their permanent home, a bit of Europe transplanted and growing in North America in the eleventh century.

No one yet has identified beyond doubt the site they chose.

The Icelandic saga describes the approach in these words: "They sailed for a long time, until they came at last to a river that flowed down from the land into a lake and so to the sea. There were great shoals outside the mouth of the estuary, and the ships could not enter the river except at high tide. Karlsefni and his men sailed into the estuary and called the place *Hóp*."

They pronounced it Hope, and we shall spell it so. *Hóp* means "Tidal Lake" or "Landlocked Bay," another clue.

There are, alas, more than a few such landlocked bays along the eastern American seaboard. One has already been mentioned—Spirit Pond, Maine, where a carpenter strolling through the wilds saw a stone, partially exposed by erosion, poking out of the bank; and then he found two more. All three bore strange markings. Perhaps Karlsefni's ships ruddered around the islands that lie off Popham Beach, then sailed up the Morse River into the shelter of Spirit Pond, which is tidal. The configuration there fits the name. What's more, one of the disputed runestones found at Spirit Pond shows the word *Hoop* and the year 1011. The sagas mention no other expedition to America during these years. But we simply don't know whether this was Karlsefni's Hope. The word on the stone is *Hoop,* not *Hóp.* Cryptanalyst Alf Mongé says he found in one of the encoded messages the date October 6, 1123, leaving us to speculate that this date might have been current, and the earlier date, 1011, commemorative.

The authenticity of the Spirit Pond stones is still an open question. There are plenty of fakes—enough to make anyone wary. There have also been genuine artifacts labeled fakes by experts. On the Spirit Pond stones we must bide our time. There are other promising sites. Much work remains to be done. "They sailed a long time" is a fragile clue to the location of Hope.

As the Norsemen looked about at Hope, they found "fields of wild wheat wherever the ground was low, and vines on all the higher ground. Every brook teemed with fish." The settlers dug trenches along the high-tide line, and when the tide went out there were halibut in the trenches. In the woods were "vast numbers of wild animals of all kinds," probably many the Norsemen couldn't identify.

On a slope above the lake the colonists claimed their acres, then burned off the grass from what would be the dirt floors of their houses and started building. "Some of the houses stood near the lake," says the saga, "and others farther away." The word in the saga is *skálarnir*: "permanent dwellings."

This land was good, and it was theirs. Or so it seemed.

They had been there half a month enjoying themselves when, early one morning, they caught sight of nine skin canoes. The men aboard them "were swinging sticks that made a noise like flails threshing, and their motion was sunwise."

Many Indian tribes are known to have used rattle sticks in their ceremonial dances. The Norsemen, keen observers, noted the sunwise motion. "What can this mean?" asked Karlsefni.

"Perhaps it's a token of peace," his co-captain answered. "Let's take a white shield and hold it up as we go toward them."

White is the universal symbol of peace—for Vikings, for Indians, and even today in the truce flag. The Skraelings recognized it, paddled in, and came ashore staring in amazement. "They were swarthy men, unattractive, and their hair was coarse," as Erik's Saga described them so many centuries ago. "They had large eyes and broad cheekbones. They stayed there awhile, marveling, and then rowed away south past the headland."

White men and natives had met in peace, inspecting one another warily, each group thinking the other weird. They probably tried a few comments that sounded like gibberish to the strangers, and then just stared in silence.

Months passed, and no more Skraelings paddled in for a look. The Norsemen got on with their work of building a settlement in the new land. Erik's Saga continues the account more simply and effectively than any paraphrase:

They remained there that winter. No snow fell, and all their livestock lived in the open and found their own food by grazing.

But when spring opened they saw, one morning early, a multitude of skin boats rowing from the south past the headland, so many that the bay looked as if it were strewn with coals. And staves were being waved on every boat.

Karlsefni and his men raised their shields, and they began to trade. What the strangers wanted to buy, above all, was red cloth. In exchange for it they offered furs and gray pelts. They also wanted to buy swords and spears, but Karlsefni and [his co-captain] forbade it. For an unblemished dark skin the natives accepted a span [about nine inches] of red cloth, which they tied around their heads. The trading went on like this for a while until the cloth began to run short. Then Karlsefni and his people cut it into strips so narrow they were no wider than a finger's breadth. But the Skraelings gave just as much for it, or even more.

To Skraelings whose garments were made of hides, cloth would indeed have been a marvel. Red cloth at that. What they gave in exchange for their red headbands that early spring morning were prime furs thick with the winter's growth, furs that Karlsefni could sell to Icelanders for a handsome price.

Next it so happened that a bull belonging to Karlsefni and his people came running out of the woods bellowing loud. This so terrified the Skraelings that they raced to their skin canoes and rowed away south past the headland.

The Icelandic saga, by its prideful silence, implies that this marked the end of the trading. And all the fault of the bellowing bull. The Greenland version adds to the record, perhaps relating what Icelanders chose to omit, for Greenlanders had, as time passed, no national pride in Karlsefni's settlement. We pick up the action in the Greenland account as the bull began to bellow:

The cattle were grazing nearby and the bull began to bellow and bawl with a terrible noise. This so frightened the Skraelings that they ran with their packs, which contained gray furs and sables and pelts of all kinds. They ran for Karlsefni's houses and tried to get inside, but Karlsefni had the doors barred against them. Neither group could understand the other's language.

The Skraelings put down their packs then, opened them, and offered their wares. Above all they wanted weapons in exchange. Karlsefni, however, forbade the sale of weapons. He hit on the idea of telling the women to carry out milk and cheese to the Skraelings. As soon as they saw it, they wanted to buy that and nothing else. So the outcome of the trading was that the Skraelings carried away their purchases in their bellies and left their packs and pelts behind with Karlsefni and his men. This done, they went away.

Now it is to be told that Karlsefni had a strong wooden palisade built around the houses.

Some time later, according to the Greenlanders' Saga, the Skraelings came again, this time in far greater numbers, bringing the same kind of wares as before. Karlsefni told the women, "Carry out the same kind of food that went so well last time, and nothing else." When the Skraelings saw it they threw their packs in over the palisade. The trading was going briskly when they heard a loud crash.

In that same instant a Skraeling was killed by one of Karlsefni's men for trying to steal weapons. Away fled the Skraelings as fast as they could, leaving their clothing and wares behind.

"Now," said Karlsefni, "we'd better get together and figure out a plan, for I expect they'll pay us a third visit. It won't be friendly, and there'll be a multitude of men."

A Skraeling had been cut down in cold blood by one of the pale intruders. A bellowing bull is frightening, but murder is outrageous. Peaceful coexistence had ended.

The first English colony in America, Roanoke, was founded almost six centuries later than Hope, but to this day we don't know for certain how Roanoke perished. By contrast, we can read how Icelanders described the battle that decided the fate of America's first white colony of record. Here is their detailed account, hand-lettered long ago on brittle parchment:

For three whole weeks there was no sign of the natives. At the end of that period, however, they saw a huge number of Skraeling boats approaching from the south like a rushing torrent. This time all the sticks were being waved antisunwise, and all the Skraelings were howling.

Karlsefni and his men took red shields and held them out. The Skraelings leaped from their boats, and the two forces clashed together and fought.

A hail of missiles came flying over, for the Skraelings were using war slings. Karlsefni and Snorri [his co-captain] saw them hoist onto a pole a large sphere the size of a sheep's paunch and blue-black in color. They hurled it from the pole up onto the land over the heads of Karlsefni's men. It made a fearful noise where it fell.

Such fear seized Karlsefni and all his men that their only thought was to get out of there. They ran up along the river, for they thought Skraelings were attacking them from every side. They didn't stop till they came to some steep rocks. There they put up a stiff resistance.

Freydis [daughter of Erik the Red] came outside. Seeing the men retreating pell-mell, she cried, "Why are you running from these wretches? Brave men like you! I thought you'd slaughter them like cattle. If I had a weapon I'm sure I'd fight better than any of you."

They paid no attention to what she was saying. Freydis tried to join them, but she couldn't keep up with them because she was pregnant. She was following them into the woods with the Skraelings in pursuit when the savages closed in on her.

In her path lay a dead man, Thorbrand Snorrason [son of Karlsefni's co-captain], with a flat stone sticking out of his skull. His sword lay beside him. She snatched it up and prepared to defend herself. While the Skraelings were rushing toward her she pulled her breast out from under her dress and slapped the sword on it.

This terrified the Skraelings. They fled to their boats and rowed away.

Bizarre as it sounds, this report makes sense in the light of the times. The battle occurred about the year 1013. Karlsefni's small band had no firearms; Europe had not yet learned about gunpowder. The Norsemen had what they thought were superior weapons: iron-tipped spears and arrows, steel swords with handsome designs on the blades, and their faithful battle-axes. They had what they thought was superior armor: round wooden shields, short coats of mail, and helmets, though only highborn men could wear helmets. The Norse, however, were accustomed to hand-to-hand combat, and the Skraelings kept hurling stones with their slings. Then the Skraelings brought out their big weapon, a primitive sort of catapult.

Many generations ago, before these sagas were known to Indians, an Algonquin chief described a similar weapon his ancestors had used "in ancient times." They constructed a demon's head, he said, "by sewing up a large boulder in a new skin. To this a long handle was tied." When the skin dried it clung tightly to the stone, and when it was painted with "devices" it looked like a solid globe on a pole. The pole was carried by several warriors who, at the crucial moment, whipped it forward, hurling the stone. "Plunged upon a boat or canoe, it was capable of sinking it. Brought down among a group of men on a sudden, it produced consternation and death."

Consternation is what it, or a similar contraption, produced among the Norsemen. They thought a second force was attacking, and they turned and ran to escape the trap. These sons of Vikings—sons of men who had terrorized Europe and gathered tribute from many shores—ran from savages who fought with stone weapons.

When the Norsemen returned to their houses and bandaged their wounds, they "pondered what force it could have been that had attacked them from the land side. Now it seemed there had been only the one force, those who came from the boats, and the other force had been a delusion." A delusion was more appalling than any weapon. It implied that the Skraelings used black magic.

Only Freydis' crazy gesture had saved them all. Except the Norseman who lay dead beside the lake and the co-captain's son Thorbrand Snorrason, who lay in the woods with a flat stone sticking out of his skull.

That flat stone may well have been part of a tomahawk

whose handle had wrenched away when the Skraeling tried to retrieve his weapon. Indians used flat stones for their tomahawks and chipped the cutting edge razor-sharp. For their slings they used round stones.

As to the other dead Norseman, the Skraelings came upon his body down by the lake as they were leaving. His battle-ax lay beside him. One of the Skraelings picked up the ax and hewed at a tree. One after another they tried it and seemed greatly impressed—until a Skraeling hacked at a stone with it, and the ax broke. A weapon that couldn't withstand stone wasn't much. They threw it away.

Even Norse pride in their weapons was shattered. Their fighting tactics, so long the terror of Europe, weren't adapted to this strange foe. And the Skraelings seemed to have magic at their command. They would come again. Their numbers had grown with every visit, and now they wanted not milk, but blood. The Norsemen were simply too few, and too far from reinforcements.

The colonists met and talked it over and reluctantly reached a decision: "It now seemed clear to Karlsefni and his people that, though the land was excellent, their life here would never be peaceful and free from fear because of the natives. So they made ready to leave, intending to return to their own country."

7
After the Battle

Soon they were gone. No ships swayed at anchor on the lake.
The doors of the houses stood open. When Skraelings entered, as we may be sure they did, they looked about in the
light that funneled down through the smoke hole and found
nothing. No more crossed swords hung on the walls, no
battle-axes, no lances, no handsomely painted round wooden
shields. Not even an iron-tipped arrow lay on the dirt floor.
 The sod houses stood empty. They would melt down and
down with the rains of centuries.

When the ships had sailed as far north as Straumfjord, the
first winter's site, there, too, the houses stood empty. Thorhall the Hunter was not waiting there to report whether he
had found Leif's cabins. For all the colonists knew, Thorhall
and his cronies might be safely home in Greenland. Or they
might be somewhere off to the north in need of help. Karlsefni knew Thorhall's intended route, if it wasn't to Greenland, so—

Karlsefni then set out with one ship to search for Thorhall
the Hunter, while the greater part of the company stayed
behind. He sailed north past Keel Cape and then bore west

with the land on the port side. There was nothing there but a wooded wilderness. And when they had been traveling a long time they came to a river that flowed down from east to west. They sailed into the river mouth and lay to by its southern bank.

There, one morning, Karlsefni's men noticed a native in an open space in the woods and shouted at him. He "came hopping down to the riverbank off which the ship lay" and shot an arrow into the ship. (If the crew shot first in vengeance for Hope they preferred not to mention it.) The arrow thudded into a Norseman who sat on the steering platform and killed him.

Karlsefni and his crew decided not to risk their lives further on a fruitless search. They returned to Straumfjord. By the time they arrived, the sailing season was far spent; so the colonists laid in provisions before the hunting and fishing failed, gathered wood for their fires, and settled in to spend another winter at Straumfjord.

Soon trouble of a different kind developed. The single men began to force their attentions on the wives. Bitter disputes broke out. The magnificent undertaking of settlement, already mortally wounded, was succumbing to human nature.

When spring came, they gathered their possessions, scythed grass for fodder on the homeward voyage, herded the cattle up the gangplank, and sailed away. "Karlsefni's son Snorri, born there the first autumn, was three winters old when they left."

Another peril awaited them at sea. A storm scattered the three ships and drove the second Icelandic vessel out into waters where shipworms attacked it. The ship was riddled, and the crew was unaware of it until she began to sink. She carried an after-boat that had been coated with tar made from seal blubber, and the shipworm doesn't bore into timber so treated. But the after-boat would hold only half the people. They drew lots, the lucky half crowded into the after-boat, and the rest, including the captain, went down with the ship. The after-boat at length reached land safely, where the survivors told this story.

Karlsefni meanwhile sailed on to Greenland, knowing only that his companion ship had not yet reappeared on the horizon. He probably returned by the same route he took outward bound, the shortest crossing, for two reasons. He knew it, and now his ship was even more heavily laden, for he was carrying not only cattle and furs but also timber. When a large *knorr* like his lay empty, her sides rose about four feet above the water, but fully loaded with heavy cargo she sailed low in the sea with only about a foot and a half of freeboard amidships.*

This brings us to another mystery—several, in fact, that build on one another.

The sagas in their laconic way report merely that Karlsefni returned safely. It would seem reasonable to infer that he sailed up Lysufjord and called again at the estate that had belonged to Thorstein Eriksson and now belonged to Gudrid. After the storm he would want to overhaul his ship before the next leg of the voyage, and meanwhile the cattle could graze in the fields. If so, was it Karlsefni who left behind there two items that might be called the most provoc-

---

*For this surprising detail—an oceangoing ship whose hull amidships rose only a foot and a half above the water—we are indebted to Olaf Olsen and Ole Crumlin-Pedersen, who reconstructed the Viking-Age *knorr* that was raised from the bottom of Roskilde Fjord, Denmark, in 1962. She was the first merchant ship of the period ever recovered, and she tells us much about the courage of those who sailed in her.

ative archaeological finds ever made in Greenland? One of them might even give us a clue to the location of Hope.

The discoveries came nine centuries later, in the 1930s, when archaeologists found the ruins of a Norse estate at the head of Lysufjord amid fields of tall grass speckled with wildflowers. The outlines of a spacious longhouse (93 by 26 feet) were clearly discernible and there were traces of a byre that once housed a large herd of cattle, other outbuildings, even a forge. Close by, down at the water's edge and visible only at low tide, lay the stone foundation of a church that once had a name: Sandnes. Behind the church was a churchyard unused since the Viking Age. Where water cut into it, bones poked from the sides of gullies.

When the archaeologists peeled back the layers of earth in the churchyard they found, buried in a grave, an Indian arrowhead. Here, three decades before the ruins at L'Anse aux Meadows were discovered, was tangible proof that Norsemen visited North America during the Viking era, for Indians never reached Greenland. At the time the arrowhead was found, some diehards were still maintaining that all sagas were fiction and no Norseman ever reached North America. Here at last was the kind of proof some people demanded: the kind you can hold in your hand.

There's more to the story, because arrowheads are often distinctive, the fingerprint of a tribe. This arrowhead, made of quartzite, might be the very one that killed a member of Karlsefni's crew while the ship lay at anchor in the river that flows from east to west. There are few such rivers along the eastern seaboard, where rivers flow east to the sea. Where was that river?

Two west-flowing rivers had been noted by avid students of the sagas, one in Massachusetts, the other in Labrador but far inland. Now evidence indicates that when Karlsefni sailed north from Hope to Straumfjord, and north again from Straumfjord, he sailed into Hamilton Inlet, the kind of bay that attracted Norsemen. Hamilton Inlet pushes deep into Labrador, then connects with Lake Melville, which reaches on west. Well over a hundred miles inland, near the lake's western end, is a river that flows from east to west. Once an ancient Indian settlement lay nearby. There in 1956 a Danish archaeologist, Meldgaard, found an arrowhead identical in shape and quartzite to this arrowhead found in the Sandnes grave. On this basis there is now wide agreement among scholars that Karlsefni sailed through Lake Melville in search of Thorhall the Hunter, and that an Indian from this ancient village killed one of Karlsefni's men.

It would follow, then, that the arrowhead buried in the Old Norse grave at Sandnes was brought there by Karlsefni. Did Karlsefni bring too the other item found at Sandnes? It was merely a lump of coal, but it might be of high importance as a clue to the location of Hope.

This lump was found in the house itself in a very deep layer as archaeologists troweled down through the centuries. In other words, it must have been placed there not long after the house was built—or, say, between A.D. 1005 and 1030. What makes it exciting is that this lump is anthracite. Greenland has no anthracite, nor has Iceland or Norway. This lump of coal was carried to Sandnes either from Europe or from the eastern American seaboard. But not from Canada. No anthracite has been found near the east coast of Canada.

Along North America's east coast, anthracite occurs in only two places. Both are in Rhode Island.

If this lump of coal was left at Sandnes as a memento from Hope, we could understand why the owner deemed it too precious to burn during all those bitter Greenland winters. (Greenlanders knew about coal and burned their own, which was of poor quality, when they could find some.)

Between Rhode Island and Massachusetts lies Mount Hope Bay, a true *hóp*: that is, a tidal bay or lake with the distinguishing characteristic of a narrow entrance. The Taunton River flows down into it from the north. The Sakonnet River flows south from it to the sea. To the west lies Narragansett Bay, connected to Mount Hope Bay by a narrow neck of water. Grapevines grow on the slopes. Anthracite lies near.

The similarity of the name might be more than coincidence. An early historian of the area who collected his data with notable care, W. H. Munro, reported that when the first English settlers reached this area the Indians were already calling it Haup or Mont-Haup, and the English merely borrowed the Indian name. Indians may also have borrowed the name. Henry Wadsworth Longfellow, writing not as a poet but as a professor of languages at Harvard, confirmed that the Indian name was Haup, pronounced, he said, exactly as *Hóp* was pronounced in Icelandic.

A few miles up the Taunton River from Mount Hope Bay, on the east edge of the river, stands a very large chunk of graywacke (a type of sandstone) known as the Dighton Rock. It is now and has been for decades virtually indecipherable and much overlaid with later inscriptions. One wag wrote on it THIS WAY TO THE SPRING. Several colonial scholars, however, saw it with fewer graffiti and found it intriguing. The Reverend Cotton Mather in 1712 wrote to the Royal Society of Antiquaries, of which he was the first American member, that there are "seven or eight lines, about seven or eight feet long and about a foot wide, each of them engraven with unaccountable characters, not like any known character." Cotton Mather was familiar with Indian inscriptions in these parts, and he also knew that Indian writing was pictographic, not alphabetic. He knew nothing of runes or Norsemen.

Two decades later, Professor Isaac Greenwood of Harvard made a drawing of the inscription and "found some difficulty; for the indentures, at present, are not very considerable, nor I think equally deep." He went on to say that "one of advanced years in the town" told him "there was a tradition went current with the oldest Indians, that there came a wooden house, and men of another country in it, swimming on the river Assoonet, as this was then called, who fought the Indians with great success. This, I think, evidently shews that this monument was esteemed by the oldest Indians as not only very antique, but a work of a different nature from any of theirs."

The wooden house swimming has the ring of truth, but its occupants were likely post-Columbian explorers, whose decked and boxy ships had more the look of a house. On the other hand, if the occupants of the swimming house had carved the inscription, Cotton Mather would not have found the characters "unaccountable, not like any known."

About 1768 a Mr. Sewell, professor of Hebrew and Oriental languages at Harvard, made a drawing of the strange characters, which baffled him, and the several figures, "very rudely executed." One of the figures was a four-legged beast, hoofed, horned, and spotted.

When the Wampanoags, Narragansetts, and neighboring tribes (all from the Algonquin language family) had been swept from the face of the earth except for a few survivors who had vanished into the woods, a copy of the inscription was shown to an Algonquin chief well versed in picture writing. He decided it was Indian, but he rejected the characters in the center of the inscription as having no connection with the figures.

So we attribute to Indians the several figures, including the horned quadruped with spots. It was not a deer, nor was it any other wild animal known in these parts in colonial times: fox, wolf, woodchuck, weasel, skunk, wolverine, or black bear. Was it perhaps a bull? Norse cattle were multicolored. Their bellowing bull was hoofed, horned, and spotted.

What are we to make of the Dighton Rock? As yet another Harvard professor, a mathematician, wrote in colonial times, " 'Tis certain it was done before the English settled in this country." Little else, however, is certain. Too many passersby have scratched too many names into its surface through the centuries. Until science finds a way to recover that first inscription, the Dighton Rock will remain a riddle.

None of this—the spotted animal with horns, the alphabetic characters unknown to learned colonials, the name, the formation, even the anthracite—constitutes proof that Hope lay on Mount Hope Bay. These are merely clues, however impressive when taken together, and other clues point in other directions. There is also a flaw, a counterclue. Thus far every theory on the location of Hope and also Vinland is marred by a flaw, though the proponents sometimes neglect to point them out. Here the flaw is that the ships would not have had to wait until high tide before entering Mount Hope Bay. It's tempting to surmise that the line "the ships could not enter the river except at high tide," described Leif's site and slipped over here by mistake, but let's play the game with the hand dealt us.

America's greatest mystery is not Where was Vinland? but Where was Hope? What site on the continent of North America did Europeans select for their first permanent settlement? Where did they build their *skálarnir*, permanent dwellings? Where was the first seed sown that might, under happier circumstances, have burgeoned into a Norse America?

8
Mass Murder in Vinland

When the frustrated settlers got back to Brattahlid with their story, Vinland became known—for a while, at least—as a nice place to visit but not to live. In the quainter words of the Greenlanders' Saga: "There was now renewed talk of a Vinland voyage, for such an expedition could bring both honor and profit."

Erik the Red's daughter, the volatile Freydis, craved both—particularly profit. Near Leif's house no one had seen a Skraeling, and Leif, too, had returned with wood.

Freydis' opportunity came soon. The same summer that she returned to the Eastern Settlement, a ship arrived in Greenland from Norway. It was commanded by two brothers, Icelanders named Helgi and Finnbogi. While they were spending the winter in Greenland, Freydis called on them and invited them to join her with their ship on an expedition to Vinland. She suggested that they share equally with her in all the profits. When they agreed, she went to her brother Leif and asked him to give her the house he had built in Vinland. Leif gave her the same answer he had given Karlsefni: He would lend the house but not give it.

Thus began the earliest known expedition to North America organized and commanded by a woman.

The two brothers and Freydis agreed that each ship should carry thirty able-bodied men, besides some women. Freydis broke the agreement by concealing an extra five men on her ship, but the brothers weren't aware of this until her ship reached Vinland.

The plan was that the two ships sail in company. There was little distance between them, but the brothers reached Vinland first and moved their gear up to Leif's house before Freydis arrived. Soon Freydis, her husband Thorvard, and her crew entered the house with their belongings.

"Why have you put your stuff in here?" Freydis demanded.

"Because we assumed," said the brothers, "that all agreements between us would be kept."

"Leif lent the house to me," she said, "not to you."

"We brothers," Helgi said, "are no match for you in wickedness." They moved their gear out and built their own house farther up on the shore of the lake, farther from the sea, and also built what was needed to make it livable. Meanwhile Freydis had her crew fell timber to load her ship.

When winter set in, the brothers suggested starting games and other entertainments to pass the time. This worked for a while, until hard feelings arose between the two groups. The games ended and visiting between the houses stopped. This lasted much of the winter.

The next incident has raised many eyebrows. You may read it as it appeared in the Greenlanders' Saga and make your own judgment:

One morning early, Freydis got up and dressed but didn't put on her shoes and stockings. A heavy dew had fallen. She took her husband's cloak and wrapped it around her, then walked to the brothers' house and up to the door.

Someone had gone outside shortly before and left the door ajar. She pushed it open and stood in the doorway for a while without saying a word.

Finnbogi, who was lying at the far end of the hall, was awake. "What do you want here, Freydis?" he asked.

"I want you to get up and come outside with me," she said. "I want to talk to you."

He did so, and they walked to a tree trunk that lay near the wall of the house and sat down on it.

"How do you like it here?" she asked.

"I like this good and fruitful country," Finnbogi told her, "but I don't like the ill will that's sprung up between us. I can see no reason for it."

"I quite agree," she said. "But my purpose in coming to see you is that I want to trade ships with you and your brother because yours is larger than mine, and I want to get away from here."

"I'll agree to that," he said, "if it will please you."

With that they parted. Finnbogi went back to bed and Freydis returned home.

When she climbed into bed her feet were cold, and her husband, Thorvard, awoke and asked why she was so cold and wet. She answered with great vehemence. "I've been to the brothers and tried to buy their ship because I want a bigger one. But it made them so angry they hit me and roughed me up. And you, you wretch, you'll avenge neither my humiliation nor your own. I can see I'm not in Greenland. I'll divorce you unless you take vengeance for this."

When he could bear her taunts no longer, he ordered his men to get up at once and take their weapons. This they did, and went straight to the brothers' house. They entered while the men were asleep, and seized them and tied them up. Each man, when he was bound, was led outside.

As they came out one by one, Freydis ordered each man killed. All the men were killed in this way. Only the women were left, and no one would kill them.

"Hand me an ax!" cried Freydis. Someone did, and she herself killed the five women and left them dead.

After this bloodbath they returned to their own house, and it was clear that Freydis felt pleased with her work. She said to her companions, "If it's our fate to come again to Greenland, I'll be the death of anyone who dares breathe a word about what's happened. We'll simply say they stayed on here when we left."

Early in the spring they made ready the ship that had belonged to the brothers and loaded it with every valuable product they could get and the ship could carry. Then they put to sea [in only the larger ship], had a good voyage, and reached Eriksfjord early in the summer.

Karlsefni was still there, his ship quite ready to sail [to Norway], awaiting a fair wind. It's said that no ship ever left Greenland so richly laden.

Freydis . . . lavished gifts on all her companions to keep her crimes secret, and then she settled down at her home. But not every shipmate kept his mouth shut, and rumors of the evil deeds began to get out. Eventually they reached the ears of her brother Leif, who thought it a hideous story. He seized three of Freydis' crew and tortured them till each confessed all that had happened. Their stories tallied.

"I haven't the heart," said Leif, "to punish my sister Freydis as she deserves. But this I predict: Her descendants will never prosper."

And it came to pass that from that time forward no one thought anything but ill of them.

This was Freydis Eriksdottir's expedition as recorded in the Greenlanders' Saga. No other expedition to Vinland has raised such serious doubts as to truth.

Certainly Finnbogi's placid consent to swap ships with Freydis reeks of fiction. But the only surviving witness to that conversation was Freydis herself, and the next conversation, between Freydis and her husband in bed, establishes how little her word was worth.

On the other hand, her entire crew presumably witnessed the slaughter. The testimony yielded reluctantly by three of her crew, each telling the same story, convinced Leif.

Or the entire tale could have been invented at some later time. One almost wishes this were the case, but it seems unlikely in the north of the Middle Ages. If some jealous, spiteful Greenlander had invented this grisly story, other Greenlanders would have rejected it, and probably rejected the author, too. The Norse sense of honor was deeply offended by lies. "Crime with words" was considered the meanest of crimes. Also, the Norse family was a unit. A stain on one name stained all, and Erik the Red and Leif were the great national heroes. Across the north a man's reputation was his dearest possession, in life and in death. Norsemen fought those they hated and sometimes killed them, but they didn't destroy an enemy's reputation with slander. Unless this tale was corroborated, it's extremely doubtful that it could have survived.

Some who accept the expedition as fact have questioned how much of the gore is for real, particularly whether a woman would butcher humans. Freydis lived in the same century as the Scottish Queen Gruach, known to us as Lady Macbeth. Scandinavia, too, had its share of violent women, as other Icelandic sagas reveal.

Freydis' voyage was the last major expedition to Vinland

recorded in any surviving saga. Only two sagas tell of the Vinland voyages, and now they fall silent on the subject.

Yet Norsemen walked again on American shores.

With no sagas to guide us, from this point on we must dig for the bits of information and try to piece them together like the shards of a broken pot.

We have been taught that the history of Europeans in early America divides into two distinct parts, Vikings and Columbus, separated by a gap of almost five hundred years. We have been told that Norsemen stopped coming here shortly after the year 1000. We have been told that by 1492 the existence of land across the sea was long forgotten, if in fact it ever was known outside the north.

In the chapters to follow, we shall examine how much of this is true. We turn now to that gap of five centuries.

9
A Bishop Sails for Vinland

When Karlsefni and his wife, Gudrid, left Greenland in that ship so richly laden, they sailed to Norway and spent the winter there. Surely in Norway they talked no less of those western lands than Bjarni Herjolfsson had, and they had much more to tell. Their audience, like his, was distinguished. "Both Karlsefni and his wife," it was noted, "were made much of by the great of Norway." Now powerful men of Norway knew about Vinland, and these were the men who owned seagoing ships, the world's finest.

They chose to do nothing about it. England was closer, and Norwegians as well as Danes were tilling their own fertile acres in portions of England each had conquered.

From Norway the news of Vinland reached Denmark, then made its way into Germany. The record keepers of the Middle Ages were, for the most part, churchmen. About 1070 a clergyman named Adam of Bremen visited the court of Svein Estridsson, king of the Danes. Returning to Bremen, Adam wrote this, the earliest written reference outside of Scandinavia to what we now call America:

He told me too of another island, discovered in that ocean by many, which is called Wineland because vines grow wild there and yield the best of wine. Unsown grain grows abundantly there, as we know, not from fabulous conjecture, but from the reports of the Danes.

Again, no flotilla of ships set out to seek Vinland. Though Thorvald Eriksson and Thorfinn Karlsefni knew it was large, no one had guessed it was half a world. In 1070 Europe was a patchwork of feudal states vying with one another. Who needed another island far out in the ocean?

Who needed another island? Possibly the younger sons in Greenland or Iceland. Iceland was "deemed to be fully settled" by 930. Younger sons needed land—wide green fields for grazing cattle. Young and old needed grain to make bread and beer; every summer the growing season proved too short for grain to ripen. Greenlanders, even more than Icelanders, needed wood to heat their homes through the long winters without resorting to peat (a spongy sod with heavy smoke) or cow cakes scraped from the stable floor.

At times their thoughts must have traveled to Vinland. Perhaps their ships did, too. The saga era, however, had ended, and the writing of history as we know it had not yet begun in Iceland or Greenland. No written record tells of another attempt to colonize Vinland. If there once was such a record, it has long since perished.

In the following century, the twelfth, at least one ship did set out for Vinland. This we know because it carried a passenger of such importance that the fact was recorded in the Icelandic Annals. The Icelandic Annals are very old historical records—lists of notable events in Iceland and occasionally elsewhere, recorded by year.

Under the year 1121, Icelandic Annals from six different sources carry this cryptic comment about Bishop Erik Gnupsson, an Icelander whose nickname was Uppsi. Here are perhaps the most tantalizing words in early American history: "Erik, Bishop of Greenland, went in search of Wineland." Or "Bishop Erik Upssi sought Wineland." In each entry, though the wording varies, the gist is the same.

The verb *leita* in Old Norse had two different meanings: "to go in search of" or "to go to give aid to." Translators invariably use the former. After all, what was there in Vinland to give aid to?

Then the records go silent, without telling us *why* a bishop sailed for Vinland, or whether he reached there, or ever returned. After the references to Bishop Erik, Vinland is never mentioned again in official records.

This is where matters stood when the Vinland Map was discovered in 1957 in a worm-eaten old volume. The map was drawn on yellowed parchment that experts believe was produced in the Upper Rhineland—probably in Basel, Switzerland—about 1440. Written on the map above a rough sketch of Vinland are these words:

> Erik, legate of the Apostolic See and bishop of Greenland and the neighboring regions, arrived in this truly vast and very rich land, in the name of Almighty God, in the last year of our most blessed father Pascal, remained a long time in both summer and winter, and later returned northeastward toward Greenland and then proceeded [back to Europe?] in most humble obedience to the will of his superiors.

In this surprising notation the least surprising information is that the Pope had heard about Vinland. Gudrid, Karlsefni's wife, made a pilgrimage to Rome after Karlsefni's death, and there were other ways the Vatican could have learned that a sizable land lay beyond Greenland. The Church was collecting tithes from Greenland and Iceland, reports were submitted, and important news traveled through the hierarchy to the top.

Let's examine more closely the official-sounding phrases. "Bishop of Greenland *and the neighboring regions*" does not include Iceland, which had its own bishops. The only other regions that neighbor on Greenland are all in North America.

The date given in the Vinland Map poses a riddle: it doesn't jibe with the Icelandic Annals. When the map states that Bishop Erik arrived in Vinland "in the last year of our most blessed father Pascal" it indicates 1117, as Pope Pascal II died in 1118. The discrepancy, 1117 versus 1121, could be explained as the mapmaker's careless error, but a sounder guess might be that there were two different visits. The first may not have included a stop in Iceland, and it may have ended when word reached Vinland that Pope Pascal had died and Bishop Erik as his personal emissary was therefore being recalled. Then there may have been a second voyage to Vinland in 1121, as noted in the Annals, with no record of his return. One source suggests that Bishop Erik died in Vinland in or about 1122; a new Bishop of Greenland was named in 1123.

Now to a crucial question. "Legate of the Apostolic See" means that Bishop Erik was appointed by the Pope himself as his personal agent. Legates of the Apostolic See are appointed for specific duties. For what specific duties did the Pope send Bishop Erik to Vinland?

Not to "sail in search of" a lost Vinland. Common sense tells us that's the task of a seafaring man with a seaworthy ship. Then to convert the natives? A bishop? A bishop with all Greenland to serve? And how could he hope to explain the intricacies of Christianity to savages without a common language?

If, however, Christian Norsemen were living in America

in the 1100s, the mission would make sense. A bishop could minister to the settlers and use them as interpreters in an effort to convert (and possibly pacify) the natives. How large a Christian settlement in America would be large enough to warrant the bishop's long voyage and provide him a reasonably secure base? Was there, in fact, a Norse colony in America in A.D. 1117?

Now the mystery deepens. When the Vinland Map came to light, Yale University called on many experts in many specialties to examine it for authenticity. They spent eight years at the task. Only the ink was not chemically tested. Tests at that time were not accurate enough for analyzing medieval homemade inks and would have required scraping away some of the writing to produce enough material to work on. Examination under a microscope indicated that the ink is not modern. The experts declared the map genuine, and Yale University published it in 1965. It was hailed as "the most exciting map discovery of the century."

Nine years later, Yale University announced that a 1974 analysis of the ink showed traces of anatase, a form of titanium dioxide first synthesized in the 1920s. Is the map a forgery?

Many are happy to relegate it to the rubbish heap of frauds and forgeries. Others believe, on the contrary, that the compound might be formed in nature and could have come into the ink used in 1440. They believe the map will ultimately prove genuine, though it might take years. Which leaves us hanging.

Those six Icelandic Annals, however, are genuine beyond doubt. As we look again at their curt testimony, we see that the same questions apply:

Would a bishop, the only bishop in vast Greenland, have sailed off to look for a lost Vinland?

Would a bishop have gone to convert Skraelings if there

had been no contacts since Karlsefni's expedition a century earlier, with no common language, not even an interpreter?

Or were there Norse settlers in Vinland in 1121, people the bishop "went to give aid to," people who could protect him from Skraelings or serve as interpreters if his mission was to convert them?

The basic question is still valid, with or without the Vinland Map: *Was there a Norse colony in America in A.D. 1121?*

This question has as yet no positive answer, no flat yes or no. No extensive ruins such as Ingstad discovered at L'Anse aux Meadows have been uncovered in a "very rich" region. There are only strange footprints on the land. We shall try to look at them with an open mind, attempting neither to make a case for the Norsemen nor to "protect" Columbus.

Eastern America has eerie echoes out of the past—hints that over a period of years Norsemen and Indians may have lived side by side in peace. One such clue is language.

When linguistics scholars began to study American Indian languages, they made a discovery that puzzled and excited them. Many words in the Algonquin language seem to have been borrowed from the Old Norse. (Reider T. Sherwin examines scores of them in his seven-volume study, *The Viking and the Red Man.*) Every language is a part of the culture of its speakers. When did Indians have such close and frequent association with Norsemen that Old Norse words were not only heard and understood but also taken into the language?

The sagas throw no light on the question. Leif saw no Indians. His brother Thorvald spoke with an ax and was answered with arrows. Karlsefni's people had only a few exchanges with Skraelings. Extended Norse-Indian contacts must have come later. Those borrowed words are echoes of unrecorded American history.

Another hint of Norse-Indian friendship is the game of lacrosse, Canada's national sport. When early French settlers in the Saint Lawrence Valley saw Indians playing it, Frenchmen tried it and liked it. Now painstaking researchers tell us the Indians acquired the game the same way—by watching Norsemen play it. The Norse called it *knattleikr*; it was their favorite game. Rough and tumble, it satisfied their need for violent sport. Several studies have analyzed, rule by rule, the similarities between *knattleikr* and lacrosse, unique among games and yet so similar to each other. One of these authors ventured the guess that "a blank chapter exists in the history of the Norse Greenlanders."

After the arrival of the Pilgrims, the land in eastern America was plowed over very early. Our pioneer forefathers never knew that anyone but Indians had walked North American shores before John Cabot. Even immigrants who arrived as late as 1837 didn't know. Rusty weapons and tools dug up in Massachusetts and Rhode Island went unexplained. Queer marks incised in rocks were assumed to be Indian doodles, and probably most were. Colonists cleared the wild land for planting, rooted out rocks, and threw them away, inscribed or not—and many were. Some were used for fences or building. Almost a hundred fifty years ago the secretary of the Rhode Island Historical Society lamented that in a short while "scarcely a vestige of them will remain."

Towns and cities began to mushroom. It's a known fact that sites attractive to one group of settlers, who presently die or move on, often attract other groups centuries later. Once in a while a homebuilder in New England dug up a weapon or tool that appeared to be Norse. But soon their significance came to be questioned: Weren't they merely mementos brought over by immigrants in the seventeenth century or later?

This charge can scarcely be leveled, however, against a tiny object found buried under a foot and a half of silt in an ancient Indian rubbish pit near the Maine coast. It's a silver coin about the size of a dime but thinner, badly worn and chipped, with a cross stamped on one side and on the other a stylized animal head, possibly a horse, though part of the nose and muzzle have worn away. Found in 1961, the coin was turned over to the Maine State Museum in 1973, where later an amateur archaeologist saw it. In 1978 he visited England and showed photographs of the coin to a noted British numismatist, who identified it as "almost certainly a Norse penny," probably dating from the reign of King Olaf III (1066–93). Another British expert concurred. "To me," he said, "there's no doubt it's a Norwegian coin struck in the 1070s."

This date eliminates all the voyagers mentioned in the Vinland sagas. They had watched American shores fade into mist behind them a half century or more before the coin existed. So reactions to this amazing pronouncement were, as they should have been, cautious. Dr. Bruce Bourque of the Maine State Museum checked out the circumstances of the discovery and reported the find authentic. The coin was taken to Norway and subjected to neutron activation analysis; it confirmed that the penny is genuine and revealed that it has a very low silver content (21.7 percent) and contains a trace of gold. The low silver content is of particular importance because it helps to narrow the time span during which the coin was brought to America. Around A.D. 1100 Norwegian pennies of low silver content were demonetized—withdrawn from circulation—and after that date those that were kept were used simply as ornaments. The coin found in Maine has a bite out of it, probably where an off-center hole was punched for stringing and the thin rim later gave way; in other words, it seems to have served as an ornament. This would have been after the year 1100, probably within two or three decades thereafter.

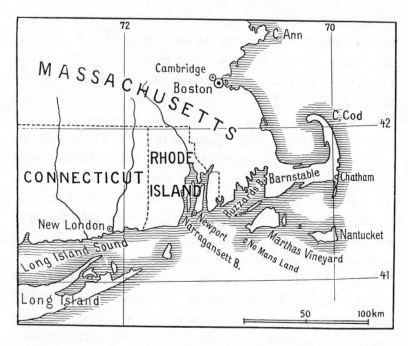

How did such a coin get to America? Someone suggested that it was inadvertently dropped at this site near Blue Hill, Maine, by a coin collector. That theory was exploded when further study revealed that this type of animal-head penny is extremely rare and is not known to have ever been in the hands of private collectors. In fact, only four examples are believed to survive, including the Maine penny.

It was also suggested that Indians might have carried it to Maine from L'Anse aux Meadows. This, however, presupposes that L'Anse aux Meadows was still occupied after A.D. 1100 and that Indians, walking or paddling, carried the coin more than a thousand miles. There's another hitch too. No medieval coins have ever been found in Greenland, though archaeologists have carefully worked the known inhabited areas. To Greenlanders, trade meant barter.

The time span points uncannily to Bishop Erik Gnupsson,

or more likely to someone associated with his undertaking. The ship he sailed in was probably the largest and most seaworthy available, which would indicate that it was Norwegian. Before we establish the bishop near Blue Hill, Maine, however, it's well to remember that Norsemen sometimes broke the monotony of a voyage by going ashore for a good hot meal. What more delightful place than here, across a finger of ocean from Mount Desert Island, one of the most scenic spots along the eastern seaboard, reminiscent of northern fjord country?

This tiny penny, while not proof positive, is a powerful indication that Bishop Erik Gnupsson's voyage to Vinland may have brought him as far as Maine or south of it.

Happily, the most intriguing riddle along the eastern seaboard is too large to move. It still stands where unknown hands once built it. You can see it today, now fenced in a park: the Newport Tower. In your mind you can sweep away recent buildings and see it as it stood long ago, on a green hill overlooking the excellent harbor of Newport, Rhode Island. What kind of ships once rocked on those blue waters?

Some claim the Newport Tower is undeniably Norse. Others claim to have proof that early English colonists built it to serve as a mill. Few structures have roused such bitter dispute.

This round stone tower stands on eight stone pillars and rises to a height of about twenty-seven feet, a modest height to modern eyes. It's unlike anything else any colonists built in America. In fact, it looks out of place here and seems to belong in medieval Europe. Its rounded arches, segmented by pillars, and the double splay are typically Romanesque. Rounded arches are a common sight in ugly old red-brick public buildings, but those were probably built in the 1890s during a brief revival of the style. True Romanesque was once the favored architectural style throughout Western Europe. Its heyday lasted a century, from about 1050 to around 1150—a time span to remember.

Who built a Romanesque tower in raw America? An answer was volunteered in the same book that informed the American people that Vikings had come to these shores. In 1837 Rafn, first translator of the sagas, declared that Norsemen built the Newport Tower. The news came as a bombshell.

The rebuttal was twenty-one years in coming. The tower, said a Harvard professor named Palfrey, was built by Governor Benedict Arnold, great-grandfather of the Revolutionary general. He built it to provide the town a windmill. In proof Palfrey offered the governor's will, dated 1677, which refers several times to "my Stone-built Wind-Mill."

With Palfrey's pronouncement the notion that Norsemen had built the tower was tossed aside. After all, why would Vikings have chosen to settle so far south? How, without firearms, could they have coped with hostile Indians? Vikings here in Rhode Island? A huge joke. And so it remained till 1942, when an archaeologist and historian named Philip Ainsworth Means wrote *The Newport Tower*.

To Means, it was the Benedict Arnold theory that made no sense. The will doesn't say Governor Arnold *built* the tower, though he probably added a windmill on top. Means learned that the tower must have been standing when white men first settled Newport in 1639. Two of the town's founders, William Coddington and John Clark, reputedly tried to find out who had built the tower by asking Indians.

As an archaeologist, Means requested permission to dig near the tower. He particularly wanted to trench out in several directions in the hope of finding old foundations that he thought extended out from it and formed a church. A church constructed in the twelfth century. He was refused permission.

A few years later, though, another archaeologist began a dig there. William S. Godfrey, Junior, excavated at the base of the tower, having been told not to trench out. As he dug, he saw that there had been at least five previous excavations around the tower. When he got down to what he believed was undisturbed soil he found two small fragments of a clay pipe such as English colonists smoked, nails, a gun flint, and a piece of glass. These, Godfrey said, dated the tower beyond all doubt as colonial.

This brought Frederick Pohl into the fray. It seemed to him that if English colonists had dug around the tower (looking for pirate gold supposedly cached there) they might inadvertently have left some of their own litter. For Pohl the question was still wide open. He kept after it till he turned up some extremely interesting facts.

Inside the tower, or windmill, is a fireplace. A fireplace that has two flues, a clue of some importance. Flues seem to eliminate all the Norse voyagers named in the two Vinland sagas, including Karlsefni. In their day, smoke had to find its own way unaided, to escape through a hole in the roof. Flues, as Pohl pointed out, were a somewhat later invention. Early flues exited through a sidewall. *These do.* They exit horizontally through a stone wall three feet thick. Not till the fourteenth century did men learn that a flue draws best when it continues up through the roof. This, said Pohl, dates the Newport Tower as no later than the fourteenth century.

He has a point. Architects do from time to time copy old styles, but they're not such sticklers for fidelity that they go to great trouble to put in flues they know won't draw well. (An American businessman recently built himself a medieval castle. Chances are it has running water and bathrooms.)

Pohl also asked: What unit of linear measure did the

builders of the Newport Tower use? Until Napoleon introduced the metric system into much of Europe, the length of a foot, a yard, a fathom differed from country to country. It occurred to Pohl that here might be another clue. As he explained it, "The measurements of spaces and openings, and widths and lengths of the constituent parts of a building invariably reveal what unit of linear measure its builders used.... What does the Newport Tower show? The stonework which its builders laid has not shriveled or swelled. . . . Its columns have not moved closer together or farther apart."

Tape measure in hand, Pohl revisited the tower and found: "Not one of these dimensions is a simple multiple of the English foot, or a simple multiple plus a simple fraction of the English foot. . . . The Newport Tower was constructed by builders who used a unit of linear measure which all dimensions show was precisely the Old Norse unit. . . . It was the unit used in Greenland. . . . The external diameter of the Newport Tower at ground level . . . is four Norse fathoms, or 24 Norse feet, which are 24 feet 8 5/8 inches, English. . . . The internal diameter between the columns is three Norse fathoms, or 18 Norse feet."

This seemed a powerful argument to answer, but the opposing faction joined in debate. The stone is rough, they pointed out, so its dimensions are hard to measure precisely. Also, units of measure varied from area to area in medieval Scandinavia. During the Viking period (though the tower is admittedly of a later date than the Viking Age, which ended about 1070), linear measurements were seldom used in construction; the size and shape of building materials determined the dimensions of a structure.

Pohl's opponents also put forward an explanation for the flues that exited through a thick sidewall and the absence of a chimney. To build a chimney stack in a circular tower, they said, would have posed a structural problem. Many continued to call the tower the Old Stone Mill and stood firm on the premise that Benedict Arnold built it in the seventeenth century.

Pohl kept sleuthing. He next went to London to examine an old document in the Public Records Office. The paper proved worth the trip.

The document was dated 1632, just twelve years after the Pilgrims sailed into Plymouth harbor. It was drawn up by Sir Edmund Plowden, who had petitioned to establish a settlement on the eastern end of Long Island. To attract settlers to this raw land, Plowden listed twenty-nine "commodities," already in existence, that his site and areas nearby had to offer. People who were considering emigrating to America were fearful of being massacred by Indians. An attack on Long Island might come from the mainland. Plowden noted that "securitie growes" if order is maintained among "the savages . . . in New England on the North." The next statement mentions "a rowned stone towre" that could house a garrison. "So that 30 idle men as souldiers or gent be resident in a rownd stone towre and by tornes to trade with the savages and to keep their ordinance and arms neate."

No round stone tower has ever been discovered on Long Island and none but the Newport Tower in "New England on the North," some forty miles away across the sound. The tower Plowden described in 1632, the tower that existed seven years before Newport was founded, could only have been, Pohl declared, the Newport Tower.

But who had built it? And when? And why?

If Benedict Arnold didn't build it (he settled in Newport in 1651), then, some suggested, English or Dutch colonials must have built it as a watchtower. This steps around the question of the round stone tower that was standing in 1632, before Newport existed, by simply ignoring the Plowden paper. Others suggested that Portuguese pirates built it. This could have put it earlier but fails to explain why pirates would have gone to such pains to imitate a medieval style.

Almost a century and a half have passed since Rafn declared that Norsemen built the Newport Tower, and no one yet has come up with a sounder solution than his, which drew laughter. The tower remains a riddle, one faction standing fast on the finds of archaeologist William S. Godfrey, Jr., the other pointing to the description of the tower written before colonists settled Newport.

If Norsemen built it, why did they bother? And why is it round?

The tower, Rafn said flatly, was built for Bishop Erik Gnupsson. Philip Ainsworth Means concurred. Both assumed that Bishop Erik came not to explore a wilderness of savages, not to look at Leif's empty cabins, but to visit a settlement of Norse Christians. A bishop needed a church. And protection from Skraelings. The Norse colonists could provide the muscle—and much was needed to haul the million pounds of stone and mortar. Engineers and artisans might have been sent ahead to supervise the work and complete the structure before the bishop's arrival.

Why is it round? Many European churches built in the Middle Ages were round, including some in Scandinavia that doubled as fortresses.

It would be a strange church—or a strange mill—that had nothing but pillars on ground level and no stairway leading up to the next floor. Yet ideal for protection. The next floor, more than twelve feet above the ground, could be reached only by ladder, and the ladder could be drawn up. The wooden interior burned out about two centuries ago, but Frederick Pohl examined the empty shell and believed he found on that elevated floor a niche for an altar table and a well recess beneath it for sacred relics. Above this floor was another room.

The windows of the tower have long been a puzzle. They're so oddly arranged for a mill—or for a watchtower. Not one window faces north, to the land side.

This fact drew the attention of an engineer, Edward Adams Richardson. After studying the tower, he published his findings in a technical journal of the American Society of Civil Engineers in 1960. Richardson reported that the windows on the top floor would enable lookouts to see ships as they approached from the east and south. The windows on the middle floor were so placed as to send out light from the tower's fireplace to signal ships to the south and east at night, when the tower itself would not be visible.

A short time later it occurred to a journalist, Charles Michael Boland, to use a method the British have employed successfully in locating Roman ruins in Britain: aerial photography. Where old foundations lie hidden under grass, an aerial photograph sometimes reveals them as lines of paler green among the surrounding grass. Using two sets of photos made in earlier aerial surveys from different perspectives, Boland placed them on a stereopticon and saw something interesting. Two light lines ran north from the tower about forty feet. They formed a rectangular area between the structure and Mill Street.

He too requested permission to dig and was refused.

None of this, singly or taken together, constitutes proof that a Norse settlement once existed near this site. The proof, if any exists, still lies in the ground. The city of Newport is currently granting no further permission to dig. If old foundations lie buried there, they must wait yet awhile. And we must wait.

Meanwhile it behooves no one to scoff at the notion of an early Norse settlement in Rhode Island. What some have called "ludicrous" may indeed have existed. History is created by people, interpreted by people, and written by people. The record is subject to change. The handmaiden of change is science.

If Bishop Erik came to America to tend a Christian flock, why didn't Europe "discover" America in the twelfth century?

To answer this, we must look at Europe as it was *then.* Most of Europe had more land than people, and as many problems as it could cope with. Countries of Western Europe were still absorbing civilization, adjusting boundaries, and gathering strength. Spain was under Moslem rule, for the Moors had swept up from Africa and conquered both Spain and Portugal. Portugal was still warring with the Moors.

During that century and the next, while the Vatican had ways of knowing of a vast, rich land across the western ocean, its urgent gaze turned instead to the East. There Moslems and Christians battled off and on for control of the Holy City, for this was the era of the Crusades. The new route to glory had its terminus in Jerusalem, a fact not lost on erstwhile Vikings.

King Sigurd of Norway early led a fleet of sixty ships from Norway through the Mediterranean to Palestine and into battle against the Turks—sixty shiploads of fighting men who might have written American history. Bloody history it would have been, but who could call the white man's conquest of America bloodless?

For almost two hundred years, from 1095 to 1272, Europe expended the lives of the bravest, the jewels of kings, and the Peter's Pence of the poor—including the poor of Greenland—in an attempt, ultimately futile, to defend the Holy Sepulcher in Jerusalem against the Moslems. To Christian Europe, Jerusalem mattered.

Vinland could wait till Europe was ready.

10
Vanished Greenlanders

After the curt notice of Bishop Erik Gnupsson's voyage, we search in vain for mention of another visit to Vinland. The likeliest source, the records of Greenland—their Annals, if any—have not survived, for reasons we shall presently understand. So we turn to other sources and leaf through volumes hand-lettered on parchment. Two centuries pass under our fingers, and the world changes. In Western Europe the Crusades have ended. Knighthood and chivalry, that other strange mix of Christian and military fervor, have flowered and are beginning to wither. In Iceland, surrounded by its moat of ocean, the enthusiasms are Christianity and literature. The oral sagas have long since been set down in writing, and Icelanders dream nostalgically of their days of glory when Vikings dominated the seas.

At last in that terse, dry record, the Icelandic Annals, we come to this small item under the date 1347:

There came a ship from Greenland, smaller in size than small Icelandic trading vessels. She came into the outer Straumfjord [western Iceland] and was without an anchor. There were seventeen men on board, and they had sailed to Markland but had afterward been driven to Iceland by storms at sea.

Only 145 years before Columbus, in other words, Greenlanders were still sailing to North America.

This was not the only voyage to America during those years, and Icelanders knew it. They knew it because Icelanders—traders, relatives, friends—visited Greenland's Eastern Settlement and carried home news. This voyage to Markland rated mention because it was unique: the little ship was storm driven over a long, rough stretch of ocean and fetched up safely, not in Greenland, but in Iceland.

The fact that Greenlanders still sailed to America was known in Norway, as well. Possibly the Vatican also knew it, if Church officials in Norway passed the word or sent the lists of tithe items that are proof of such visits. Tithes collected from Greenlanders were sent to the archbishop in Norway. Few Greenlanders could pay in silver now. Their best cash product, the ivory of the walrus tusk and narwhal horn, was inferior to elephant ivory from Africa; and besides, ivory was going out of style. So the Pope had instructed the archbishop to accept whatever Greenlanders could give and sell it in Norway. The items were duly recorded. The archbishop's Greenland list includes the furs of seven animals Greenlanders must have obtained in North America: for example, the black bear. Greenland itself had only polar bears.

Not only were Greenlanders poorer now. They faced a truly major crisis: a deteriorating climate.

The human race fondly believes it shapes its own destiny, but through the eons climate has shaped the lives of all living creatures. Scientists tell us a warm period such as we now enjoy is the exception, not the norm. The last great Ice Age lasted more than fifty thousand years and ended before written history. The warm spells between ice ages, the "interglacials," are thought to have lasted about ten thousand years. Our present warm spell, having favored us for almost ten thousand years, seems to be nearing its end. If we were to chart our balmy interglacial, however, even this line would sawtooth. Its peaks mark warm periods such as the present, and its valleys indicate "little ice ages." One of these began in the thirteenth century and grew more intense as the years passed.

As early as about 1250 the author of the geographical treatise *Konungs Skuggsjá* (The King's Mirror) described ice that appeared in what had previously been open water: "Sometimes these ice fields are as flat as if they were frozen on the sea. . . . Sometimes they lie quiet . . . at other times they travel with a speed so swift and violent that a ship with a fair wind behind it is not more speedy; and . . . as often against the wind as with it. There is also ice of a different shape which the Greenlanders call icebergs."

In the Western Settlement, hundreds of miles farther north than the Eastern, farmers began to notice that the grass was frost killed earlier. (Similarly today, in England, the growing season is said to have shortened by two weeks since 1936.) In Greenland, harvesting enough grass to feed the stabled cows through the winter had always been a struggle. Even in the best of times the half-starved cows grew so weak they had to be carried bodily out of the stable when the first grass greened in the spring. Now winters were even longer, and cows were shut in the stable sooner.

When the temperature falls gradually, as it did, people at first make small adjustments. Greenlanders moved the cow barn in and connected it to the house. Manure has warmth. Not only Greenlanders changed their habits in the worsening climate. As the sea itself grew colder and pack ice moved south off Greenland's west coast, sea animals too moved south. Groups of Eskimo hunters followed. Greenlanders met Eskimos for the first time in Norðrsetur about 1266 and thought them primitive. "They lack iron entirely and use the tusks of walrus for throwing weapons and sharp stones for knives."*

Norsemen called the Eskimos Skraelings. Indians or Eskimos, what did it matter? To proud Norse eyes they seemed the same—dark, disheveled, "inferior" people, different from Europeans.

The Norse found the Eskimos to be of a friendly nature, and the two peoples seem to have got along. It may have been shortly after this time that they started trading. If a Norseman ever vented his bloodlust, Eskimos would not have banded together to seek revenge. It was not their way.

And still the climate worsened. Only by another degree or so, but where living is marginal a drop of a few degrees can be perilous. The herds of the Western Settlement dwindled as cattle starved. The westerners, reluctant to slaughter their surviving cows and put an end to milk and cheese, more and more had to seek their meat by hunting.

Winters lasted so long that no wood could be spared to fuel the forges. Merchant ships rarely came, so there was no new supply of iron. When a ship was wrecked, Greenlanders drew out every nail. But nails don't shape into arrowheads without heat, and arrowheads were essential to hunting. Greenlanders began to carve arrowheads from bone. Bit by bit, circumstances were pushing them back to the primitive, turning them into ironless hunters like the Eskimos.

---

*This observation was passed along to Norwegians, who wrote it down in *Historia Norwegia*, probably the only reason it has survived.

Still ice pushed relentlessly farther south, animals moved south, and again bands of Eskimo hunters followed. By about 1342 they had reached the Western Settlement.

When word of this came to the Eastern Settlement, the lawman at Brattahlid sent a group of men to the Western Settlement to oust the intruders. Among those who went was the priest Ivar Bardsson, sent over the previous year from Norway. His report on the mission was brief:

When they came there they found no man, neither Christian nor heathen, but only some cattle and sheep running wild. They took as many of these as the ships could carry, and sailed back.

The Western Settlement's ninety farmhouses and four churches stood empty. Every occupant had vanished. To this day no one knows where they went, those six hundred or so people who simply disappeared. They were not massacred by Eskimos; Ivar Bardsson mentioned no bodies, no signs of battle, no charred ruins. Yet the eastern Greenlanders seem to have known their western cousins would not return, or the rescue party would not have carried away the cattle.

Almost three centuries later, Bishop Gisli Oddson sat at his table in Iceland and tried to piece together from scraps the records destroyed by fire a few years before, in 1630. For the year 1342 he wrote:

The inhabitants of Greenland of their own will abandoned the true faith and the Christian religion, having already forsaken all good ways and true virtues, and went over to the people of America [*ad Americae populos se converterunt*].

"The inhabitants of Greenland" refers here only to the Western Settlement. Their "sin" had been to extend the hand of friendship to Eskimos. The Church of the fourteenth century strictly forbade contact with heathens. Three centuries had passed since Karlsefni's people had traded with Skraelings. Meanwhile the Crusades had stirred devout Christians all over Europe and even as far out as Iceland to hate the infidels—and anyone else who didn't hate them. To make friends with a heathen and trade with him as a friend was to forsake good ways and true virtues.

In this lonely land the Greenlanders' sense of being part of the civilized world stemmed in large measure from the Church. Humiliated and ignored by the Church and no longer able to feed their families by dairy farming, the western Greenlanders may indeed have turned to "the people of America."

But which people? North America had both Indians and Eskimos. For generations these words have puzzled historical sleuths as they tried to sift through the clues and discover what went on in America before Columbus.

Some believe the western Greenlanders abandoned their unproductive farms and took up hunting as their way of life. Sooner or later, so this theory holds, the westerners joined the wandering Eskimos and presently intermarried. Eskimos knew how to stay alive in a cold climate.

Others maintain that the Greenlanders crowded into their few remaining ships, took as many cows and sheep as they could spare room for, if any, and in the tradition of their ancestors sailed away west-over-sea. In a kinder land they could try again to live like civilized Europeans.

There are scattered clues that both guesses are right. The ice pack at any given time may have determined the route. No need to assume that every family agreed on the same decision. Or even left at the same moment. We shall look at some of these clues.

The people of the Western Settlement were pioneering types. Wilderness didn't dismay them. Distance was just an inconvenience. Norsemen had not only voyaged to Vinland. They had already explored the whole bleak length of Greenland—some two thousand miles—to reach the northernmost shores of the earth.

We know this despite the absence of written records because they built eider houses, small stone structures to protect eiders' nests, on Ellesmere Island off Greenland's far northwest corner. Eiders, large northern ducks, line their nests with softest down. Later the Greenlanders returned to the nests and gathered the down so their wives or mothers could make warm, lightweight eiderdown quilts—but only as long as they had sheep to supply wool for the shells.

This points to another puzzle as we begin our search for the vanished Greenlanders. There are traces over a wide area of North America—hints that Norsemen may have been there. But which traces were left after the Western Settlement was abandoned, and which before? Which were left by travelers out of the Eastern Settlement? Or by Europeans after Columbus?

After quitting the Western Settlement, some Greenlanders may have moved west and north for better hunting, leaving their herds behind. Eskimos, to be sure, had moved south to hunt sea mammals, but Norsemen preferred the meat of land animals. West of Greenland, across Davis Strait, lies Baffin Island in northeast Canada. We have already noted its marvelously rich hunting grounds. When a Dutch ship visited Baffin Island in 1656, the crew were amazed to see blond Eskimos.

In this bitter-cold region, colder even than Greenland, the Norsemen would have found that the type of clothing worn by Eskimos afforded better protection. Besides, without sheep there was no more wool. The American explorer Vilhjalmur Stefansson, who lived north of the Arctic Circle for an unbroken period of more than five years, learned that the rigors of Arctic existence can be much reduced by adopting the Eskimo way of life.

These hypothetical Greenlanders probably picked up the Eskimo language too, for Eskimos could teach them much. Eskimos had trekked about the top of the world and could have told Greenlanders that each year vast herds of caribou migrate across the central Arctic. In far northern Canada, up where a maze of islands dots the central Arctic, stone structures have been found that, some contend, were winter shelters for Norse ships.

Adopting the Eskimo way of life might have been a large step toward the assimilation of ex-Greenlanders. Stefansson reported that on Victoria Island, halfway between Greenland and Alaska, he saw among the Eskimos three men "whose beards were almost the color of mine." (Both of Stefansson's parents were Icelanders.) These three Eskimos looked, he said, "like stocky, sunburned, but naturally fair Scandinavians." Other explorers have encountered the same type scattered through the central Arctic, even a few Eskimos with blue eyes.

Their presence has given rise to the theory that the people of the Western Settlement were ultimately absorbed by the Eskimos. Probably some were, but we can't assume that every family that left the Western Settlement headed into the Arctic.

Some may have turned their prows toward Labrador, then down its long, bleak coast and across the narrow Strait of

Belle Isle to northern Newfoundland. Newfoundland lies at the mouth of a mighty river, the St. Lawrence. Glance a moment at the map on page 71. If you follow the Newfoundland coast in either direction and keep following it, you'll presently enter the Gulf of St. Lawrence, the gateway to the river.

Follow that mighty river inland, and you enter the Great Lakes. Long before locks or canals were built, you could sail from the Atlantic Ocean to the westernmost end of Lake Superior, the westernmost of the Great Lakes, a distance of 2,350 miles. You could do it with only a bit of hauling—a few miles around Niagara Falls and the rapids above, of course, and a few miles around several other rapids or falls. Norsemen had the strength to drag their ships overland and did so. The worn bottom on the Norse *knorr* brought up from Roskilde Fjord is silent testimony to this.

In a wilderness, traveling by boat is easier than on foot. Vikings from east-facing Sweden had learned this in Russia, where they followed rivers and lakes across that vast land. When necessary, the Swedish Vikings had heaved their ships onto log rollers and dragged them overland to the next river till they came eventually to Constantinople, and some went on into Asia. No need for us to assume that refugees from Greenland's Western Settlement clung to American coasts, unable or unwilling to venture inland.

The question is not *could* they but *did* they sail into the Great Lakes? Early farmers plowing their fields near the Great Lakes turned up objects that looked to be Norse. A few of these are still around. Now tests are available that could determine the age of the metal, the general type of processing, and the source of the ore.

An archaeologist, however, wants to study an artifact *in situ*—in the ground, snugly encased in layers of undisturbed earth. Only then can the soil tell him how long the object has lain there. Without this proof there is always the suspicion that the artifact was planted centuries later. An archaeologist explores with trowel and whisk broom instead of a plow. In many places he arrives too late.

Some who deserted the dying Western Settlement may never have reached the St. Lawrence. They may have sailed across to Baffin Island by skirting the lip of the ice and then sailed southward off Baffin Island's grim shores and entered the first great waterway they came to. We call it Hudson Strait.

Almost two hundred miles into Hudson Strait, on a peninsula on the southern coast of Baffin Island, archaeologists in 1977 made an interesting find. In a circular house once occupied by Thule Eskimos, its roof made of whale ribs covered with sod, they were digging down through two feet of soil and refuse. At the bottom, on the stone slab floor, they came to a tiny figurine only 2 1/8 inches tall: a Greenlander. "The significant fact about this figure," said Michigan State University anthropologist Moreau S. Maxwell, "is that it was carved by a Thule Eskimo and represents a European man. It provides concrete evidence of contact between Europeans and Baffin Island at a very early date."

How early? The clothing tells. There's no longer a helmet (and there was never a helmet with horns except for certain rituals). This figure shows a man wearing an ankle-length hooded robe. Three experts have identified it as a typical Norse costume of the thirteenth century. By the fourteenth century, hoods had developed tails—the liripipe hood we know through portraits, such as the one of Chaucer. Of course, off in the Western Settlement, where merchant captains no longer cared to risk cargo and ship amid the ice, the isolated residents may never have learned that the style had changed.

Whether this Greenlander came to America before the main exodus from the Western Settlement or with it, one fact seems evident. The Thule Eskimo who carved the figurine had more than a distant or passing glance at him. Carved in this tiny piece of wood are intricate details: a cross suspended on the chest, a yoke running between the shoulders, two vertical seams from yoke to crotch, and another line circling the hem at the ankle—proof of close contact.

To other Greenlanders, the southern shore of Hudson Strait looked more inviting. Coasting along it, they came soon to Ungava Bay, which takes a deep bite out of northern Quebec. At the foot of this bay caribou grazed. There in 1965 archaeologists uncovered a village built in the Middle Ages and believed to be Norse. They found ruins of houses with thick sod walls (though not so thick as in Greenland, where walls were often six feet thick). They found cairns, which are heaps of stones such as Norsemen erected to mark trails that might be obliterated by snow, and fragments of two soapstone bowls that must have been carried over from Greenland.

Greenlanders of this period weren't accustomed to congregating. There were no cities or towns in Greenland then and none in Iceland. Some of the villagers may have pushed on, still following the water route inland. The map shows in bare outline the route that lies open before a voyager who sails deeper into Hudson Strait.

Hudson Strait leads into Hudson Bay. If Norsemen entered Hudson Bay and began coasting down and around its shores, they would have passed the mouths of many rivers. Some are small, some large and inviting. Several could have carried a shallow-draft vessel to a network of rivers and lakes that cover a wide span of Canada and reach down into the United States.

Centuries later, in 1803, President Jefferson sent Lewis and Clark to explore unknown territory just acquired in the Louisiana Purchase. The expedition started from St. Louis and sailed up the Missouri River. By the second winter they had voyaged as far as an Indian village near the present Bismarck, North Dakota, and spent the winter among Mandan Indians. These Mandans were an enigma to the explorers. They seemed typical Indians. In fact, they were called, in sign language, "the tattooed people." Yet their houses and mode of living suggested extended contact with more civilized people. The Lewis and Clark expedition reported that some of the Mandans had blue eyes and blond hair.

Lewis and Clark were not quite the first to reach these parts. The first white man known to have entered North Dakota was a French-Canadian explorer, the Sieur de la Vérendrye. Seeking a water route from the Atlantic to the Pacific, he had followed tributaries of the Red River of the North (the Assiniboine and Souris) till he came in 1738 to the Missouri River in North Dakota. There in the territory of the Mandan Indians he found what was described as "a large stone, like a pillar, and in it a smaller stone was fixed which was covered on both sides with unknown characters. This stone . . . was about a foot of French measure in length and between four and five inches broad."

The French-Canadians asked the Indians who wrote the inscription and in what language. But all the Indians could tell them was that the stone had been there "since time immemorial."*

---

*This account is from the diary of Professor Peter Kalm, a member of the Swedish Royal Academy of Sciences, who visited Quebec and received a report of the incident from Captain Vérendrye himself and "heard it reported by others

The explorers broke the inscribed stone loose and carried it away with them.

Its strange symbols so impressed Pierre la Vérendrye that when he made a trip to Quebec five years later he carried the stone along and handed it over to some Jesuit scholars for scrutiny. Like Vérendrye, the Jesuits were familiar with Indian pictographs and knew that the alphabetic characters on the stone were not the work of Indians. Neither the Jesuits nor Vérendrye knew anything about runes. The Jesuits were also unable to read the inscription. They compared it with illustrations of Tataric inscriptions in books in their library and thought the characters looked "perfectly alike."

The Tatars, or Tartars, were originally a nomadic people who roamed in Asia and Europe, but they were never seafarers. Tataric characters and Norse runes look much alike; eight, in fact, are identical, and others are remarkably similar.

All agreed that the mysterious inscription must be important. So the stone was sent to Paris, to the Minister of Colonies. There it disappeared.

If the Vérendrye Stone ever reappears and if it should prove to be a Norse runestone, it might be easier for some to believe a strange message carved in another stone, called the Kensington Stone, found far inland. Meanwhile, the Kensington Stone remains one of the two most controversial objects attributed to Norsemen.

---

who have been eyewitnesses of everything that happened on that occasion."

11
Were Scandinavians in Minnesota in the Middle Ages?

In 1898 a farmer named Olof Ohman was clearing a wooded hill on his farm about two miles out of Kensington, Minnesota, so he could plow. Ohman, a large and powerful man, grubbed out trees by digging a trench around a tree to cut the horizontal roots and then used the tree itself as a lever to pry it out. When he felled one aspen whose trunk was eight to ten inches thick he saw that a large, rectangular stone was enmeshed in its roots. When he had cut the stone loose and turned it over, so the story goes, his ten-year-old son, Edward, noticed strange marks on it. Ohman was a Swedish immigrant who had bought this farm eight years before. As a boy he had learned the runic alphabet, and he recognized these marks as runes.

Word spread around the neighborhood, and for a time the stone was displayed in a shop window in Kensington. No one who saw it could read its message, including Olof Ohman, who had had only nine months of schooling. One man copied the inscription and sent it to a Swedish-language newspaper in Minnesota. The newspaper got around to publishing it two months later. A copy of the inscription was sent to a professor of Scandinavian languages at the University of Minnesota, O. J. Breda, and the brouhaha began.

Professor Breda, though not a runologist, translated part

of the inscription. He couldn't decipher the date or any of the numerals, but he got the gist of the message. It was sensational. Swedes and Norwegians, it stated, had camped near there on a journey west from Vinland.

From Vinland? To Minnesota? The professor knew that the Vinland sagas mention no Swedes or Norwegians in Vinland and no journeys far inland. What he didn't know was that the inscription was dated three and a half centuries after Leif's time. To the professor, Vinland implied Leif Eriksson, but the language of the inscription wasn't Leif's Old Norse. Some of the words weren't even in use yet around the year 1000. The inscription seemed to contain Swedish, Norwegian, and English words. Professor Breda declared it a fake.

He also sent a copy of the inscription to two professors at the University of Oslo, Norway, and published their reply. They pronounced the stone "a grand fraud perpetrated by a Swede with a chisel and a slight knowledge of runic characters and English."

The finger seemed to point at Farmer Ohman. He had found the stone, and he owned a book that contained a runic alphabet. He lugged the stone home in embarrassment and dropped it at the entrance to his granary, face down, where it served as a doormat for eight years. There was still no complete translation, but in the minds of the public the inscription had been condemned by experts as a clumsy fraud.

In 1907 a young man named Hjalmar Holand, a student of Old Norse literature, saw the stone and was so interested that Ohman gave it to him, happy to be rid of the thing.

Holand worked out a complete translation. On the face of the stone, which is 36 inches long by 15 inches wide, he read this message:

[We are] 8 Goths [Swedes] and 22 Norwegians on [an] exploration journey from Vinland round about the west.

We had camp by 2 skerries one day's journey north from this stone. We were [out] and fished one day. After we came home [we] found 10 [of our] men red with blood and dead. AVM [*Ave Virgo Maria*, Hail the Virgin Mary], save [us] from evil.

Apparently the carver intended to sink the stone as a gravestone, for only the top half carries runes. There was more to say, however, and the message continues on the edge, which is six inches thick:

[We] have 10 men by the sea to look after our ships 14 days' journey from this island. Year 1362.

The reference to "this island" is explained by the fact that Ohman found the stone on a knoll in an area that had been a shallow lake until white settlers drained it.

The date 1362 shook a good many people. It wiped out many of Professor Breda's objections. Others found it beyond credibility. Swedes and Norwegians in Minnesota 130 years before Columbus reached the West Indies? No way.

The Norwegian Society of Minneapolis wasn't going to be taken in by a hoax. It appointed a committee to investigate circumstances of the discovery. This is what they learned.

The neighboring farmer testified that he had seen the tree many times. When the stone was removed he saw that the roots "were flattened on their inner surfaces and bent by nature in such a way as to exactly conform to the outline of the stone. I inspected this hole," he said, "and can testify to the fact that the stone had been there prior to the growth of the tree." Five others in this small community, where each knew his neighbor's character, testified that they, too, saw the tree's flattened roots.

The committee established that the trunk of the aspen tree

was eight to ten inches in diameter. Dendrologists, scientists who specialize in trees, calculated that in that climate it would take an aspen tree about sixty-nine years to grow to that size. The tree had stood there with the stone in its roots since about 1829—more than twenty years before the first translation of the Vinland sagas was published and hence before the public was aware that any Europeans reached America before Columbus.

Geologists, too, examined the stone and reported that the weathering of the inscription must have taken at least fifty to a hundred years and probably much longer. Even fifty years would date the carving before any Swedes or Norwegians settled in Minnesota.

This combined testimony would seem to rule out a prankster, but now other questions were raised. It's difficult to judge the age of a buried inscription because normal weathering doesn't occur. Some simply rejected the geologists' report. What proof was there beyond the statement of Ohman and his son, they asked, that the inscription wasn't added after the stone was removed?

Runologists in particular refused to accept the inscription. If it's genuine, they asked, why are there so many errors in the text? Why does it include runic forms not in use in 1362? Why does it include words not in use in Norway or Sweden in 1362?

Others asked: What would Swedes and Norwegians have been doing in America so late—almost 350 years after the last voyage recorded in the sagas—and yet 130 years before Columbus?

Why would they have gone so far inland?

Hjalmar Holand decided to try to answer these questions. In fact, he devoted the rest of his life, more than fifty years, to the riddle of the Kensington Stone. In his research he came upon a letter written by Magnus, king of Norway and

Sweden, in 1354. Here, said Holand, is the key to the riddle.

First, a word about King Magnus. He was an ardent Christian whose major purpose in life was to convince the Greek Orthodox Catholics of Russia—by force of arms—to accept the Roman Catholic Church. To achieve this, he personally led two military campaigns into Russia. Both failed. Then the Pope offered King Magnus half the tithe money collected in Norway and Sweden to preach a holy crusade. King Magnus was planning a third invasion of Russia when word reached him that the plague, the devastating Black Death that had ravaged Norway a decade earlier, was raging in Russia. King Magnus' army refused to go there. And here he was with all that money.

The people of Greenland were his own subjects, for fading Greenland had surrendered her independence to Norway. Magnus knew that the people of the Western Settlement had gone elsewhere, "having already forsaken" Christianity. As their king, he may have thought it his duty to restore them to the faith—now that he had the funds and couldn't use them in Russia.

We can only guess at the motives behind it, but the letter he wrote is a fact. By this letter, dated 1354, he commanded Paul Knutsson, one of the leading men of Norway, to organize and lead the expedition. Paul Knutsson was ordered to select officers and men he thought best qualified, including members of the king's bodyguard. The king added:

> We ask that you accept this our command with a right goodwill for the cause, inasmuch as we do it for the honor of God and for our predecessors, who in Greenland established Christianity and have maintained it until this time, and we will not let it perish in our days. Know this for truth, that whoever defies this our command shall meet with our serious displeasure and receive full punishment.

A royal command such as this was scarcely to be ignored. Paul Knutsson's expedition is believed to have sailed from Norway about 1355. Almost nothing is known about it. In 1364 a ship with only eight survivors aboard returned from Greenland to Bergen, Norway. Some see, in those eight survivors, all that remained of the royal expedition.

The expedition would have sailed first to the Eastern Settlement and found it still there and still devoutly Christian. There Paul Knutsson would have tried to pick up what information he could on the whereabouts of the vanished western Greenlanders. Then what?

Between, say, 1356 and 1362 there was ample time to look for the erstwhile Greenlanders in America—to search for them far more extensively than Karlsefni once searched for Thorhall the Hunter. There was time to search down along the east coast, then backtrack northward, still searching. There was time to sail through Hudson Strait, a route almost certainly known to Greenlanders by that time, and so into Hudson Bay. There was time to sail across Hudson Bay or instead to skirt its long coastline and sail south and west up rivers that looked inviting but only led them deeper into the wilderness. (Except for one wrong turn where a river forked, they might have found the Mandan village in North Dakota.) Between 1356 and 1362 there was ample time to reach Minnesota. No surviving letter, however, records either King Magnus' gratitude or his disappointment, or reports where the expedition went.

Many charge there is not one crumb of proof that the Paul Knutsson expedition reached America. Holand believed that the message on the stone provided the proof. In truth, the Paul Knutsson expedition *is*, at this stage, only a theory. The Kensington Stone, on the other hand, we can see and feel. The men who carved its message may have come solely to explore. The inscription calls the mission *opdagelsefard,* which could be translated "exploration journey" or "journey of discovery." So the controversy circles back to this: Is the inscription genuine?

This is a battle of experts—runologists, linguists, philologists. Even they disagree among themselves. We can't hope to follow all the arguments, but a couple might indicate the drift. One word the critics questioned was *dead*, spelled *ded* on the stone. There is no such word in Old Swedish, said the critics. The perpetrator of the hoax, they charged, not only dropped in an English word; he didn't even know how to spell it. Holand, however, searched old records and found a letter written in the fourteenth century by Queen Margaret of Norway, Sweden, and Denmark in which she wrote the word *ded*.

Other "English" words that prompted scholars to label the inscription a childish fraud are *of, mans, illy* (evil), and *from*. All have since been found in Scandinavian writings of the fourteenth century. Details such as these have led some to conclude that it's easier to accept the Kensington Stone as authentic than to believe that a nineteenth-century prankster could have put it all together.

The geography too has been challenged. It would have been impossible in the fourteenth century, critics rightly point out, to sail from Kensington, Minnesota, to the Atlantic in fourteen days. Holand, however, believed "the sea" where the rest of the party waited was not the Atlantic but Hudson Bay.

He visualized Paul Knutsson's ships anchored on the west shore of Hudson Bay at the mouth of the Nelson River. A search party, he theorized, took a boat and followed the Nelson River southwest to Lake Winnipeg, then down across Canada through Lake Winnipeg to the Red River of

Holand's Reconstruction of the Route

the North, which forms the present boundary between Minnesota and North Dakota. From the Red River, in Holand's reconstruction, they sailed into its tributary, the Buffalo River, and followed it to a north–south waterway that has since vanished. Today innumerable lakes dot Minnesota in a band running roughly south from the Buffalo River to Kensington. Holand believed they once formed one lake, an unbroken waterway of sufficient depth for sailing.

To cover the 1,050 miles from Hudson Bay to Kensington in fourteen days, the vessel would have had to average 75 miles a day—half the distance a Norse ship at sea averaged in a twenty-four-hour day. This journey, if it was made, apparently was undertaken in the fourteenth-century version of an after-boat, or so we might infer from the message on the edge of the Kensington Stone.

Others have noted that Lake Superior lies within a fourteen-day journey from Kensington. To one who has never seen such a lake, Superior's great size would suggest an ocean. Holand, though, wanted everything accurate and defensible. The word *hawet*, he pointed out, means "salt sea," which Lake Superior is not. Hudson Bay is a true inland sea.

Though Holand's theory on the route sounds farfetched, the disturbing fact is that of all the Norse-looking objects dug up in the Midwest in the last century or so—swords, spears, axes, halberds, fire steels—by far the greatest number were unearthed near this route, some before and some after he propounded his theory. We'll glance at a few of these puzzling objects.

In 1870 a group of men set out to look for farmland in an uninhabited part of northern Minnesota. Well beyond the last homes of settlers they came to Cormorant Lake and decided to stop and fish from shore. While the father cleaned fish, his ten-year-old son poked a hand into a crevice between two large rocks and found a small fire steel. At the time it was merely a curiosity, a puzzle. Decades later, it gained significance when the Kensington inscription was translated. Still later, Holand learned that several fire steels of precisely the same size and ornamentation are preserved in the museum of the University of Oslo, and these are known to date from the Middle Ages.

The following year the same family moved farther north in Minnesota and became the first white settlers in Polk County. That year, 1871, the same boy was playing along the west bank of the Red River at a point where its bank was eroding, when he saw a handle sticking out about two feet below the grassy surface. He dug it out and found the handle mineralized and the blade broken. The strange object, it turned out, was a halberd. A halberd is a battle-ax mounted on a shaft. The shaft continues several inches beyond the ax blade and ends in a spearhead. (You've seen Vatican guards holding these symbolic weapons.) Halberds were a symbol of royal authority.

The charge has been leveled that all the rusty old weapons and tools dug up along the Red River and in various parts of Minnesota have turned up as the result of the search for evidence to support the Kensington Stone. The Kensington Stone, however, didn't appear till 1898, and some of these finds, including the two just noted, were made earlier.

It's certainly true that many appeared after. Some introduced a fat red herring, and one find in particular dramatizes the confusion.

On a point of land that jutted out into Lake Darling about three miles north of Alexandria, which is near Kensington, a St. Louis woman had a summer home. One summer she decided to have her driveway changed. Workmen cutting down trees for that purpose found a rusty halberd about three feet underground, entangled in the roots of a very large oak. In 1923 she gave the halberd to an interested neighbor.

Now to the red herring. About 1890 the American Tobacco Company introduced a new tobacco plug and wanted a catchy name for it. They had heard about these peculiar artifacts that had been dug up in Minnesota and were sometimes mistakenly called battle-axes. So the new tobacco plug was named the Battle Axe plug. To advertise it, the company sent merchants a cutting board with a small halberd hinged to it. The ax blade could be lowered to cut the plug. When the campaign ended, some of the merchants detached the fake halberds and put them to other uses, decorative or practical. Years later some of them were found, rusty or even buried, and were mistaken for small ceremonial halberds from the Middle Ages.

The Lake Darling halberd, many charged, was just another tobacco cutter. This so annoyed Hjalmar Holand that in 1944 he sent it to Professor R. A. Ragatz, Chairman of the Department of Chemical Engineering at the University of Wisconsin, for chemical analysis. With it he sent a halberd found at Frog Point, and later he sent a third halberd. Professor Ragatz analyzed the metal of the three and found the Lake Darling halberd and the halberd from Frog Point genuinely medieval, and the third a cheap and late imitation.

A few years ago the Lake Darling halberd was back in print again. A respected archaeologist whose opinion was based on the similarity of form wrote: "This 'halberd' is in reality nothing more than a tobacco plug cutter from the latter half of the nineteenth century."

A viewer's opinion of these objects seems often to reflect his acceptance or rejection of the Kensington Stone. There are now, however, dependable scientific tests available that analyze metal without consuming too much of the object, tests that tell whether its composition is medieval or modern. This is the kind of information the historian needs in order to reconstruct history from fragments.

The authenticity of these artifacts does not depend on the Kensington Stone. Nor does its authenticity depend on them. Holand's route too, dotted though it is with such finds, can be accepted or rejected without proving or disproving the authenticity of the stone. There are many ways a man with a boat could have reached Minnesota. In the 1700s, when the British and French were colonizing eastern North America, this area west of Lake Superior was the scene of a keen trade rivalry between Britons and Frenchmen bartering with Indians for furs. Though still wilderness and far inland, it was not too far for a man with a ship because of two great waterways. English traders came south from Hudson Bay. The French came west through the Great Lakes or adjoining rivers. Norsemen might have come to these parts by either route.

Whether they did is a decision for historians of the future. The Kensington Stone will stand tall in that decision. So any development, any new method that might help establish whether its inscription is genuine or a hoax, assumes major importance.

Now we might have one: cryptanalysis—as exciting as a spy story.

Cryptanalysts see their work as a tool for solving old riddles, opening new horizons, and discovering dramatic chapters in the past heretofore undreamed of. Most runologists, on the other hand, doubt that cryptanalysis can be applied to runic inscriptions.

Cryptanalysis means, of course, the solving of messages written in cipher or code. As used here, the term refers to a special type of cryptogram found hidden in runic inscriptions. The skill to compose this kind of cryptogram and even the knowledge of its existence were lost for more than five centuries. The rediscovery came about like this.

In the 1930s a distinguished runologist at the University of Oslo, Professor Magnus Olsen, was studying medieval runic inscriptions that included a few symbols not in the runic alphabet. It occurred to him that these "tree runes," as they're called, might be signals planted by the rune-master to alert the reader to look for a message hidden in code. From this tip-off Magnus Olsen solved the first runic cryptogram and read the secret message.

About thirty years later cryptanalyst Alf Mongé discovered that some rune stones whose inscriptions seem straightforward and contain no tree runes also have hidden messages. One of these, he maintains, is the Kensington Stone.

A word about Mongé's qualifications: Alf Mongé has devoted his life to cryptanalysis. As a cryptanalyst in the U.S. Army Signal Corps he succeeded in breaking one of the Japanese enciphered codes shortly before World War II. In March 1966 he wrote to a friend, O. G. Landsverk, that "preliminary study of the Kensington inscription tends to indicate a possible connection with other medieval cryptograms—a connection so fantastic that, for the moment, I refuse to believe it."

Before the end of the year he believed it. He had deciphered the secrets hidden in the text of the Kensington Stone.

Deciphered, the Kensington cryptogram reads: "Harrek made me." (That is, Harrek composed the message and devised the cryptopuzzle.) "Tollik cut me." And the exact date: Sunday, 24 April, A.D. 1362. The importance lies not in these few words but in their implications.

Harrek, if Mongé is right, was almost certainly a priest. The literate class was composed largely of clergy, for monasteries were the schools of the Middle Ages. In Scandinavia the clergy continued to use runes. Priests and monks accompanied groups who set out on hazardous missions. Harrek, moreover, was probably a Benedictine. Benedictines were then predominant across northern Europe, and the Christian Church in Norway, Iceland, and Greenland was almost exclusively Benedictine. It was Benedictines who in medieval times indulged in the intellectual game of composing cryptograms, then dating them in code to confirm their authenticity.

The medieval science is called "calendrical cryptography." As Mongé explains it, each rune was associated with a number, just as to us C might represent 3. The calendar the Benedictines used—and the calendar used in composing the Kensington cryptogram—was the Roman Catholic Ecclesiastical Calendar. This was the Julian "Old Style" calendar that went out of use in Norway in 1700 and in Sweden in 1753. In addition to having a Julian calendar, the Kensington rune-master also had to have, as Mongé puts it, "certain Julian Calendar Easter Tables used almost exclusively by the Roman Catholic clergy."

A hidden message is useless unless something signals a reader to look for it. Harrek, Mongé believes, introduced deliberate misspellings. Sometimes the same word is used twice in the same way but spelled differently. Such errors led twentieth-century runologists to doubt the Kensington Stone's authenticity. Harrek altered the shapes of some of the letters, and this too led to the charge of fraud. These changes, these apparent errors, says Mongé, were introduced not only to attract attention. They are essential to the solution—*to make the count come out right.* Solving a cryptogram is a process in arithmetic.

Runologists are rarely cryptanalysts, and there's the rub. The two groups don't yet speak the same language. Most runologists refuse to concede that history lies buried in such a puzzle. It's a game, they say, that could be used to produce a secret message in Mongé's own book. Mongé considers the dated cryptogram of the Kensington Stone positive proof that the inscription is genuine. For these reasons:

The art of composing dated runic cryptograms was lost for five hundred years. It was still unknown in 1898 when the Kensington Stone was discovered. This fact, Mongé maintains, eliminates absolutely the possibility that the Kensington message could have been composed as late as the nineteenth century. Or in the eighteenth, or in any of the intervening centuries back to the years before Columbus.

Since the secret of dated runic cryptograms was rediscovered and solved in our century, others from medieval times have been deciphered in runic inscriptions found in Norway, Sweden, Greenland, and, yes, in Oklahoma, near a tributary of the Mississippi.

If Swedes and Norwegians were in the Midwest in 1362 they may have been exploring, or they may indeed have been searching this wilderness for refugees from the Western Settlement. If so, what reason for believing the refugees might be found in Minnesota? Why would displaced Greenlanders have pushed on west when America's east coast or the St. Lawrence Valley offered all they needed and their ties lay in Greenland and Iceland?

Like a detective seeking a motive for crime, a historical detective tries to understand what needs or yearnings motivated people in their movements. A fascinating theory has been proposed recently by James Robert Enterline. He suggests that Greenlanders may have pushed west because they mistook America for Asia.

Too weird to believe? Columbus, remember, mistook America for Asia and perpetuated the error by naming the natives Indians.

Try a moment to look at it through the eyes of a Greenlander who has abandoned his home in the Western Settlement because he could no longer feed his family there. He chose not to move to the crowded Eastern Settlement. (This seems obvious, else Ivar Bardsson's crew would not have sailed from the Eastern Settlement to rescue the Western.) He chose not to return to Iceland, having heard that there, too, conditions were bitter. His ship was small, possibly for lack of nails. It might have been as small as the ship that was storm driven to Iceland in 1347. Norway, the land of his forefathers, lay far over the sea, across its stormiest and foggiest expanse. Vinland was closer.

He may have settled at first near the eastern American seaboard, but soon realized that no ships from Europe would call there. He and the others who had chosen to sail southwest were alone in a wilderness. In the three and a half centuries since Karlsefni he had heard tales of great waterways leading inland to richer hunting grounds or wider fields.

As he penetrated deeper into the American wilderness, he became aware that this was a landmass, not a mere island. It wasn't Europe or Africa. So didn't it have to be Asia?

Asia was little more than a name to him—the easternmost part of what was believed to be earth's one landmass. He knew that Vikings had sailed from Sweden through Russia to Asia. If the world is a globe and there's only one landmass, Asia must lie west of Greenland. He had no notion of Asia's size. If he could sail west through Asia, he may have reasoned, he might come in time to Russia, then maybe at last to Norway.

This theory, too, is bound to be controversial. It assumes that these fourteenth-century Norsemen believed the earth is a sphere. Perhaps they did. Perhaps they had learned it from Eskimos who had trekked around the top of the world. Or perhaps, as a seafaring people, Norsemen had deduced it themselves, in this way:

When mountains fell away astern, they seemed to sink into the ocean until only the peaks were visible. Why? Because the earth itself curved? When a ship appeared in the distance, the sail showed first, and later the hull. Why? Because the earth curved? For centuries Norsemen had steered by the North Star and noted that it stood higher in the sky when the ship lay north, and lower as observed from more southerly waters. Why? When Europe was calling the earth a flat disk, Norsemen said it was humped like the back of a turtle. Already in those early years they had grasped the idea that the earth is not flat. In the intervening centuries, combining their own observations with those of the wandering Eskimos, they could well have developed this idea to its logical conclusion.

The possibility that Greenlanders might have been pushing west through America to reach Norway, though still without proof, grips the imagination. It foreshadows the efforts of many later explorers who sought the Northwest Passage, including the Sieur de la Vérendrye, who in 1738 hoped to sail from the Atlantic to the Pacific by way of North Dakota.

Ever since it became public knowledge that Norsemen found America five centuries before Columbus, the popular view has been this: it scarcely matters where Greenlanders went. Greenland was cut off from civilization, so nothing came of these efforts.

Greenland, however, was not yet cut off from civilization.

True, news of the western Greenlanders' deepest penetration into America was probably not carried back to the Eastern Settlement. Still, *some* information as to their whereabouts seems to have reached the Eastern Settlement. How else to account for that cryptic entry in the Icelandic Annals that the Greenlanders "went over to the people of America"?

In the year assigned that entry, 1342, the Eastern Settlement was still alive. Its four thousand or so people were still in contact with continental Europe and still capable of passing the word along.

Five years later, five years after the Western Settlement lay deserted, people of the Eastern Settlement still visited the mainland of North America. That small, battered ship from Greenland that fetched up in Iceland in 1347, storm driven after visiting Markland, could have come only from the Eastern Settlement, the living link between two worlds.

12

A Portuguese-Scandinavian Puzzle

A century before Columbus reached America, the lands of Western Europe presented a strange contrast. Part of the sleeping giant was beginning to stir.

For nine hundred years, ever since the fall of ancient Rome, monks cloistered in monasteries had kept alive the flickering flame of learning by copying old manuscripts and teaching young clerics and the sons of noblemen to read and write—but not to think. Now at last the light of learning was casting its beam beyond cloistered walls. Universities were springing up. With the dawn of the Renaissance, the horizons of knowledge were pushing out, stretching wider like fields at sunrise. And more than learning was coming to life.

Ideas were aborning—ideas that would lift Europeans out of the treadmill of centuries. Individual expression and worldly experience gained new importance. Nations and city-states were gathering strength. Trade flourished, bringing contact with other cultures and new ideas along with the products. There was contact with Moslems, and much to learn from them in mathematics, astronomy, and medicine. Even the making of paper, today indispensable, was an art Europeans learned from the Moslems, who in turn had learned it from the Chinese. And now at last Europe itself had contact with China and the mysterious East.

The Orient became more than a name when the Polo brothers, Nicolò and Maffeo, and Nicolò's son, Marco, returned from a twenty-four-year trading visit to China, Sumatra, and other lands on the far side of the world. Back home at last, the three travelers ripped open the seams of their shabby coats, and out tumbled diamonds and rubies, emeralds and sapphires. Merchants realized then that the East was the place to go. Europeans were developing an appetite for luxuries, and merchants were eager to feed it. Caravans trudged ten thousand miles across desert and mountains to reach those fabulous treasures.

By contrast, people across the north still plodded along in the medieval rut, and few had ever savored luxury. Scandinavia was held fast in the grip of the little ice age. There the quality of life was deteriorating, and so was trade. Norway's trim, low ships had lost out long since to the boxy, high-sided, square-ended ships of other nations, particularly of the Hanseatic League, that joint commercial enterprise, and England. Their clumsy ships could carry more cargo in their deep bellies, so they gobbled up trade that once had crossed in Norwegian hulls.

When Norway suffered Greenland suffered, for Greenland had yielded her cherished independence to Norway in order to keep ships coming. But the Royal Norwegian *knorr*, which had been dispatched twice each year to Greenland, sank and was not replaced. Norway, her list of customers shrinking, refused to let other nations trade with Greenland.

As if that wasn't trouble enough, the ice pack off Greenland's west coast was still creeping south. Eskimos reached the Eastern Settlement. Often what we fear the most—if it comes—proves least offensive. According to an Eskimo account handed down by word of mouth, some of the Eskimos wanted to live among the Norsemen, but the Greenlanders forbade it and permitted them only to trade. As the ice continued to creep south, the Eskimos moved on with it to Cape Farewell, and from there on up the east coast.

And Greenland was still in touch with the civilized world.

We know of a ship from Iceland that landed in Greenland in 1406 and stayed four years, probably because ice prevented the ship from leaving. We know of this visit because back home in Iceland the visitors described an elaborate wedding they had attended in Greenland, impeccably Christian from the first calling of the banns through the reading of the nuptial mass.

Official records mention no ships to or from Greenland after 1410. Yet still ships arrived from Europe.

When sails next appeared far down the fjord and Greenlanders ran to the quay rejoicing, they soon learned that the foreigners hadn't come to trade. They were pirates. They pillaged the churches, where the few treasures Greenland possessed were housed, then burned the churches. The roles of pirate and victim were now reversed from the days of the old Viking sea raiders. Most of these pirates, though by no means all, came from England. They stormed into the churches as Christians, whereas the old Vikings had worshiped pagan gods and the objects they stole held for them no religious meaning. The latter-day pirates may even have used strange weapons that spurted death, for firearms at last had come into use in Europe.

When the pirates departed they carried away many Greenlanders, particularly the huskiest, locked in the holds of the deep-bellied ships, to be sold in Europe as slaves. Iceland, too, was ravaged by pirates. Now people whose national memory included Vinland, Hope, and whatever followed were scattered through northern Europe.

Pirates came again and again to Greenland. When the raids began, in the first half of the fifteenth century, the Eastern Settlement had a population of three or four thousand people. Their grandfathers and possibly some of these very people had voyaged southwest to Markland for wood. Some may now have decided their chances would be no worse against Skraelings than against civilized Europeans. There are hints in the reports of later explorers that some of these Greenlanders did actually move to eastern Canada half a century or more before America was officially discovered in 1492. But there is no proof. No written records have ever been found in Greenland.

As to the captive Greenlanders who were dragged off to Europe as slaves, a matter of record, did none of them talk? Not one? Did nobody tell about Vinland or Hope or even Markland?

If somebody talked, it would scarcely have mattered. It's doubtful that even one merchant captain would have turned his prow toward Vinland to discover America and gain renown everlasting.

Traders sail for profit, and Vinland had nothing Europe needed.

Europe had its own wood and grapes. Furs could be fetched with less effort from Russia. What Europe wanted was gold and silver, silks and spices, perfumes and precious stones. Spices disguised the flavor of meat half rotten for lack of refrigeration. Perfume masked the smell of the human body when bathing was rare.

All these delectable items could be found in "the Indies," which meant not only India but most of eastern Asia, including Japan and China. Something, however, had gone amiss. Caravans no longer trudged across Asian desert and mountains. The Turks had captured the Balkans and stood defiantly blocking the caravan route.

Still, there was a way. A merchant could sail east through the Mediterranean and proceed to Mecca, that great Arabian market city where goods of the East and West changed hands. He could gaze on rows of eastern luxuries laid out for barter and take his pick. He could watch a procession of camels humping into the city laden with spices they had lugged from the farthest reaches of Asia.

The bonanza ended in 1453 when the same "beastly Turks" captured Constantinople and gained control of the eastern end of the Mediterranean. Soon its waters swarmed with Turkish corsairs bent on capturing Christian ships and settling old scores from the Crusades. The route to the riches of the Orient had been cut by Turkish sabers.

To us today the solution seems simple—just time-consuming. Why not sail around Africa to Asia, as our oil tankers did in recent years when the Suez Canal was closed? In the mid-fifteenth century, though, Africa was a land of mystery: the Dark Continent. No one knew how far south it extended or if, in fact, it ended. No one knew whether the crew would die gasping in fiery heat or be scalded in steaming waters when the ship sailed through the torrid zone. The world had forgotten that two thousand years earlier those ancient mariners the Phoenicians had sailed completely around Africa. In the fifteenth century, men pondered whether it could be done.

One man decided to try. Prince Henry the Navigator, prince of Portugal, had the wealth and power to gamble and the will to learn. Each year he sent out Portuguese caravels with instructions to sail down the African coast, round it, and find their way to Asia. The caravels pushed a little farther each time before turning back, but always more of Africa still lay ahead to the south. Prince Henry died in 1460, and still the Portuguese kept on trying.

Presently a few men began to wonder if there was an easier route: a route that would lead to the very source, to the Spice Islands themselves and the land of the Great Khan, China.

Merchants had earlier reported that an ocean lay to the east of China. Could it be the same Great Ocean that lapped against Western Europe? Then why not sail west to the Golden East? The earth is a sphere.

In the enlightened fifteenth century, educated men all over Western Europe accepted the fact that the earth is round. American schoolchildren used to be told that Christopher Columbus was the first to present the idea. There was even a foolish story about his breaking an egg to prove it. Yet a century before Columbus, the poet Chaucer wrote this line in Middle English: "This wyde world, which that men seye is round. . . ." The wonder is that so many students have read that line in recent centuries and asked no questions. Actually, the idea came first to the ancient Greek Aristotle, who perceived it three centuries before the birth of Christ. Aristotle noted that the height of the polestar differed when he traveled north or south, and from this small observation he deduced that the earth is a globe. Now ancient Greek learning had been revived in an awakened Europe. True, in the fifteenth century the masses still spoke of the four corners of the earth and were sure it was flat. But many knew better.

Then why not sail west to the Golden East? The answer was easy—and known even then. The earth's circumference, its girth at the waist, had been calculated at very close to the true figure. Asia was much, much farther from Europe than a ship of that era could sail across empty ocean before the crew died of starvation or scurvy.

But what if the coast of Asia extended farther east? What if those merchants who saw it long ago underestimated Asia's enormous breadth?

Again the Portuguese tried to find out. In fact, they had been trying for decades to learn the secrets of the "Sea of Darkness," the Atlantic. Step by difficult step they pushed slowly westward. They had discovered the Azores a third of the way across the Atlantic and started to colonize them. If they attempted to sail west from the Azores, as they surely must have, they would have encountered powerful head winds and currents that held them back.

We don't know how the Portuguese learned that farther south, on the latitude of northern Africa, trade winds filled the lateen sails and blew a ship steadily westward. Perhaps a caravel sailing near the Canary Islands was caught in one of the fierce storms out of the east that are common to that area and was driven west, and then the friendly trade winds carried the ship along.

Whether by calculation or chance, far west of the Canary Islands the Portuguese found that strange phenomenon we call the Sargasso Sea, which lies in the western half of the Atlantic. Here, for hundreds of miles, dense seaweed grows on the water. The Portuguese named it the Mar de Baga, or Berry Sea.

Beyond this seaweed sea they found more. They found an island or chain of islands they named Antillia. Antillia first appeared on a map in 1424. The map still exists. Provocatively, the name Antillia is a compound of two old Portuguese words meaning "island in front of."

Many modern historians call Antillia a mythical island, but one of the great cosmographers of that era, Toscanelli, was firmly convinced of its existence. It was Toscanelli who, in his old age, advised Columbus where to sail. If a prankster sketched Antillia on that early map, he was fortunate indeed to select a location where that rarity, a chain of islands, dots the Atlantic. We call it the Antilles, the West Indies.

After finding Antillia, the Portuguese lost it. They found it again, and lost it again.

In the search for lost Antillia they learned that the Sea of

Darkness is vast and empty. The voyage pushed superstitious seamen to the very limit of their courage, and some turned back. And Asia was nowhere in sight.

Toward the top of a globe the circumference shrinks to a fraction of its girth at the waist. Anyone can see that. Up north, then, the eastern and western rims of earth's landmass should lean closer together across a narrower ocean. The Portuguese understood this.

They knew, too, that people had sailed southwest from Greenland and come to a land or several lands out in the Ocean Sea. Many historians agree the Portuguese had heard about that. Not only did Portuguese ships make regular runs to Bristol, England, whence Bristol ships made regular runs to Iceland and once in a while to Greenland. Lisbon itself was at this time the world center of nautical science and the city of mapmaking. It was the crossroads where sailors from many countries tarried and talked of their travels; and their information was diligently collected.

The Portuguese also knew that up north the ocean provided an important aid that is lacking farther south: stepping-stones—rest stops where the crew could take on food and water. Iceland, Greenland, and then that land southwest of Greenland—the last known rest stop before a crew pushed on west in search of China.

This brings us to a strange story. At present it can be called no more than a story, entitled "The Lost Voyage to America." But it might yet become history as specialists sift and weigh the evidence that exists in fragments found in many countries and turn up more in their patient sleuthing. Or it might be filed forever in the morgue of unsolved cases.

The key piece of evidence didn't come to light until 1909, when the owner of a very old letter decided to make it public.

The letter was written in 1551 by Carsten Grip, burgomaster of Kiel, to King Christian III of Denmark. It reads:

> I have this year seen a map found in Paris showing your Royal Majesty's land, Iceland, with a description of all the strange things to be seen there . . . and it further states that the two skippers Pining and Pothorst were sent out with several ships by Your Majesty's grandfather, Christian I, at the request of His Majesty the King of Portugal, on an expedition to the new islands and the continent in the North.

This expedition to "the continent in the North," if it occurred, preceded Columbus' voyage. Christian I, king of Denmark and Norway, died in 1481.

The letter linked at last a number of baffling references found on old maps and in old state papers, telling of Portuguese and Scandinavian explorers in North America in the 1470s. Sometimes the names of João Vaz Corte-Real (Portuguese) and John Scolvus (Scandinavian) lie close together on the same old map. Guided by this letter that reappeared after three and a half centuries, some researchers now believe there was only one expedition, this joint effort, Portuguese and Scandinavian. King Alfonso V of Portugal, they theorize, conceived the idea and financed the expedition. At his request, the Scandinavians provided their knowledge. Pining and Pothorst, for example, knew Greenland waters, having operated there as pirates.

If we start with this premise of a joint effort, which the letter mentions, and piece together the scattered references like a jigsaw puzzle, a fascinating picture emerges. Examine this reconstruction with care before you decide to accept or reject it.

In this theoretical reconstruction, the joint expedition embarked in 1476 or a year earlier. They sailed first to Iceland. The letter establishes that. Their next step would have been Greenland, then on to the mainland of North America. The letter takes them that far. Where next?

If they followed Karlsefni's example and sailed across Davis Strait for a narrower crossing (though farther south, skirting the ice), their first glimpse of North America would have been Baffin Island. As they sailed down along its bleak coast, João Vaz Corte-Real, King Alfonso's observer and personal representative, watched for a gap, a water route to the west that might lead through this land and out to the ocean on the other side. It would signal itself by a powerful current.

At the mouth of Hudson Strait they encountered a tremendous current and enormous tides, among the world's highest. As they scanned the horizon to the south, they saw not the faintest shadow of land. The ships bore west and sailed into Hudson Strait.

There is evidence for this, too. An English state paper of about 1575 lists all early attempts to find the Northwest Passage. The one it records as earliest: "On the north side of this passage was John Scolvus, a pilot of Denmark, in 1476." No question but that "this passage" was what we call Hudson Strait. The same state document calls it "the swift ronning downe of sea into sea"* and tells us that to find it "we must sail to the 60th degree." Hudson Strait lies at 61° North latitude.

Sailing through Hudson Strait, the ships came into Hudson Bay. The lord lieutenant of Newfoundland, Baron de Lahontan, wrote in the 1600s that Henry Hudson had seen

---

*Norwegians knew of this strait long before. The Norwegian geographical treatise *Konungs Skuggsjá* (The King's Mirror), written about 1250, tells how water pours through the strait from the Inner Ocean to the Outer Ocean.

a "memoir" of a Danish voyage into the bay and made his own voyage into it as a direct result. (Hudson's discovery of Hudson Bay in 1610 gave England her claim to the Hudson Bay region.) The lord lieutenant goes on to say that the expedition wintered on a shore of Hudson Bay, where "savages" provided them with food and furs. His evidence is shakier than we would like because he got the name and date wrong, but authorities on Henry Hudson believe the Danish explorer referred to was John Scolvus. A little later John Oldmixon in his *British Empire in America* referred, somewhat sniffily, to a claim that "a Dane made the discovery of this Streight and named it Christiana, from the King of Denmark." Dare we assume the king was this same Christian I?

For explorers seeking a route through to the western waters, Hudson Bay was a blind alley. The ships turned back. At the mouth of Hudson Bay they turned south. After all, they weren't looking for polar bears or an ice-clogged passage. So they sailed south along Labrador. Here are some of the clues:

The Spanish priest Francesco Lopez Gómara, writing of Labrador in his *Historia de las Indias* in 1553, said: "Here too have come people from Norway under the leadership of Captain Juan Scolvo [John Scolvus], and the English under Sebastian Cabot." The Dutch author Cornelius Wytfliet wrote in 1597: "But the honor of America's second discovery belongs to Johannes Scolvus *Polonus* [a corruption of *pilotus*], who in 1476 sailed into the northern strait under the Arctic Circle, and came to Labrador. . . ."

The Portuguese rated mention here, too. A map of Labrador in an atlas by Vaz Dourado in 1571 shows a point of land labeled *Teso de João Vaz* and a bay marked *B. de João Vaz*. João Vaz Corte-Real was a Portuguese officer in whom King Alfonso placed great trust, and his rank in the expedition must have been high. Old maps show no fewer than six American sites bearing his name.

As they sailed on south, the next great opening that would have lured them in was the swift-flowing Strait of Belle Isle (the strait between Labrador and Newfoundland). On a globe made about 1537 by Gemma Frisius with the help of Mercator we find, in the Strait of Belle Isle, this touching inscription: "Through here the Portuguese tried to sail to the Orient, the Indies, and the Spice Islands."

The Strait of Belle Isle leads a voyager straight into the Gulf of St. Lawrence. On the same globe this comment stands north of the Gulf of St. Lawrence: "The Quii people, to whom Johannes Scolvus penetrated about 1476." The "Quii" might have been a corruption of Cree. Cree Indians, reputedly warlike, lived in these parts at that time.

Here the westward trail ends. The ships may have sailed on up the St. Lawrence River; or the leaders may have foreseen only endless days of more wilderness and more hostile natives.

Sooner or later they had to backtrack and exit from the Strait of Belle Isle. At its mouth they seem to have turned south once more, this time along Newfoundland. If they followed its coast, they would have met with a final frustration, for Newfoundland is an island. Its southern coast would only have led them back into the same Gulf of St. Lawrence.

If, instead, they followed the southern shore of the St. Lawrence River on their return and exited through its southern gateway, they may have discovered Cape Breton Island, just north of Nova Scotia. South of that, each inlet to the west would have led them to another dead end, and we have run out of these names on the old maps.

In the following century, geographers knew Newfoundland, Cape Breton Island, and the adjacent continent by a

Portuguese name, *Terra do bacalhao,* which means the "land of stockfishes." A Portuguese historian, P. Antonió Cordeiro, in his *História Insulana,* mentions the return of João Vaz Corte-Real "from the land of stockfishes, which they had gone to discover by order of the Portuguese king."

When João Vaz returned to Portugal and sailed into harbor, no cheering thousands welcomed him at the dock. King Alfonso V probably wrote off the expensive enterprise as a failure. The expedition had found no waterway through to the Orient. It found only the Helluland-Markland-Vinland complex long known to Norsemen.

Only these and similar scraps of information imply that a joint expedition, Portuguese and Scandinavian, visited America about 1476—sixteen years before Columbus and twenty-one years before John Cabot. Did the expedition really occur?

In reconstructing history, the historical detective today is confronted with two factors that pull against each other. Historians of earlier centuries were less fastidious about facts. Some of their history is based on rumor, some is corrupted by errors, and once in a while an account was blown up like popcorn from a kernel of truth. On the other hand, much pure history went unrecorded; or records were lost over the centuries, or still lie undiscovered, moldering in cluttered archives.

One crucial piece of evidence for this expedition is still lacking: There is no official record. Trade routes were the road to riches, and the Portuguese of the fifteenth century jealously guarded the secrets of their explorations and generally did not publish the results. Instead, only one copy of a report was written. It was submitted only to Prince Henry the Navigator or, after his death, to King Alfonso.

So specialists themselves disagree. The eminent geographer Dr. Bjørnbo, for example, argued that there must have been an official report on this expedition, and it either has been lost or still lies buried in some record office or library. The distinguished historian Henri Harrisse, on the other hand, expressed grave doubts on the validity of some of the evidence. Here, then, we have a glimpse of historical detectives at work with the raw materials, gathering and sifting evidence and weighing it like jury and judge.

If eventually this expedition is validated, it will demonstrate another phenomenon: the unimportance of North America to men who sought instead the fabulous wealth of the Indies.

It's a sobering thought that in this category were not only King Alfonso but also Christopher Columbus and John Cabot.

Late in 1476, when João Vaz returned to Portugal (if in fact the expedition occurred), Columbus was living in Lisbon. His work at that time was making maps and sea charts, and he gathered data for them by talking with seafarers who had just returned from distant places. A few months later, so his son Ferdinand reported, Columbus took ship to Iceland. Those who knew him described Columbus as a man who was always asking questions. In Iceland he may have learned nothing. Or he may have had his suspicions confirmed that the large land out in the ocean was only a wooded wilderness—and much too far north to be the Indies. Or it may have been in Iceland that he formed his lifelong obsession that Asia lay within sailing distance.

John Cabot, who walked where Norsemen once walked, wanted only to stand in the presence of China's Great Khan. His story began to build to a climax before Columbus sailed for the Indies.

13
Vinland Rediscovered

Outside Scandinavia, the English were in the best position to pick up word of Markland or Vinland as the Age of Discovery drew nearer. English fishing boats speckled the ocean off Iceland. English merchantmen regularly carried wares from Bristol to Iceland, and English sailors went ashore and mingled with Icelanders. Sometimes merchant ships out of Bristol even called at Greenland. True, Norway forbade it, but merchant captains knew the watchdog had grown feeble.

When the whole Western world became aware of the Vinland sagas less than a century and a half ago, people were amazed that America had been discovered twice. Voyages to Vinland around the year 1000 were so remote in time from Cabot's discovery in 1497, however, that there seemed no possible connection. Knowledge of Vinland, it was assumed, was lost when contact with Greenland was lost. Historians knew that John Cabot said he met a Portuguese sailor who had visited Greenland in 1492. They shrugged it off as a tall story.

Now archaeologists—those historical sleuths who rewrite history with a trowel—have uncovered proof that merchant ships out of Europe visited Greenland from the days of Erik the Red down into the final triumphant quarter of the 1400s, the "Age of Discovery."

At Herjolfsness, the cape Bjarni Herjolfsson's father named for himself, archaeologists found the ruins of an ancient churchyard on the lip of the sea. Digging there, they uncovered the bodies of fifteenth-century Norse men and women, many with a small wooden cross in their hands. The clothes of the dead in the upper layers, the latest burials, had been miraculously preserved because permafrost rose and the ground around them stayed frozen summer and winter. Styles change, and clothes can be dated. The clothes told the story.

The dead were clothed not as Vikings, but in long, full woolen robes such as Europeans, both men and women, wore in the late Middle Ages. There was also a hat—a Burgundy hat, tall, brimless, flat crowned, like a section of stovepipe covered in black cloth. These ludicrous Burgundy hats were worn by style-conscious Europeans when Columbus had grown to manhood. The archaeologist who exhumed this hat from a Greenland grave, Poul Nørlund, called it "a very important document . . . testimony that as late as toward the sixteenth century there were ships going to Greenland from Europe."

Stretches of years must have passed when not one sail came out of the east. And then one day a ship would appear, grow larger, close with the shore, and drop anchor. Some ships came from England, especially Bristol, and probably a few from other countries, including Portugal. All stopped to rest at Herjolfsness, the first harbor after the long crossing and still some distance from the heart of the Eastern Settlement.

Sea dogs love to talk of the sea and far places, and here at Herjolfsness were tangible items to turn the discussion to Markland. The archaeologists found thirty-two finely constructed wooden chests—so many that they must have been items for trade. The chests were made of fir, spruce, and tamarack. The tamarack could have come only from North America, probably from Newfoundland or Labrador.

Bristol merchants may have listened to talk of Markland with no compelling surge of interest. England had her own wood. They probably consulted their rutter, a book of sailing directions to many lands, and found no mention of Markland or Vinland. They may have looked at their sea charts (though England had fewer maps than southern Europe, where the art was further advanced) and found neither name.

Sea charts showed several islands out in the ocean that sounded far more enticing—Antillia, Brasil,* St. Brendan's Island. Antillia was usually shown in the far southwest, opposite northern Africa and near the western edge of the chart—too far from England. Brasil and St. Brendan's Island seemed to drift about.

One day a merchant saw a map that showed Brasil in a new position: southwest of Ireland. We might speculate that the chart maker had moved that drifting island northward because, in this age of secrecy and rumor, he had heard whispers of a Portuguese-Scandinavian expedition to a land of stockfishes, which we call Newfoundland. But this is sheer conjecture.

Brasil, now, that was worth some thought. Brasil was said to abound in spices.

As the merchants mulled it over, trying to visualize what might lie in that empty ocean, they had cause to remember Markland. Could Brasil be that island or land that Greenlanders knew positively was out there? Greenlanders in their

---

*Spelling was fluid in those days. Brasil has been spelled Brasylle, Brazilli, Brazir, Brasile, Bracir, Bersil, and possibly other ways we've overlooked.

little ships had called there and returned home safely. It could be done. Brasil, the isle of spices, lay within sailing distance.

The efforts that followed imply that several English merchants were certain Brasil was no mythical island. Brasil was for real. It was out there southwest of Greenland. But why sail northwest to Greenland, into the ice, and then south again to Brasil? Why not follow the base of the triangle?

In the summer of 1480 two merchants of Bristol sent out a couple of ships to search for "the Island of Brasylle on the west part of Ireland." The ships were commanded by Thomas Lloyd, "the most scientific mariner in all England." He beat his way westward, often into the teeth of the wind. He seems to have had no clear notion of the distance west from England to the isle he sought. For nine weeks he saw nothing but ocean. Then storms forced the ships to abandon the search.

In other summers other ships sailed out of Bristol, skirted the southern coast of Ireland, and held west. They found nothing. And yet they were learning much—the prevailing winds at different seasons, the currents, the ways of the western sea.

Meanwhile, in Venice, an Italian named Giovanni Caboto, whom we know by the anglicized form of his name, John Cabot, was dreaming dreams. He dreamed of buying eastern goods at their source (he called it Cathay and we call it China), where the price would be right. He had heard that Cathay's hundreds of cities lay on rivers navigable from the sea. He knew, however, that Turkish corsairs swarmed in the eastern Mediterranean. And he knew from his time in Lisbon that Africa still stretched on and on. . . . If a ship could sail west across the ocean, the voyage would be shorter . . . quicker . . . and safer. . . .

It may have been about this time that he moved his family and his dreams to England. Nobody knows exactly what year he arrived—or why. In fact, we know little about John Cabot. No scrap of his writing remains. We know only what his contemporaries said he believed and what can be deduced from his actions. He may have heard from a friend that Bristol merchants were sending out ships to seek land to the west. Italians were then the cosmopolitans of Europe, and many lived in England. England would be a good place to embark on his mission—up there where the girth of the globe is smaller. . . .

March of 1493 brought Europe momentous news. Christopher Columbus had set out from Spain, sailed down to the Canary Islands, and then run west before the trade winds across the ocean until he came—so he said—to the Indies. In the spring he returned to Spain, bringing six "Indians" in full paint and ornament, and was welcomed by cheering thousands.

One who didn't join in the celebration was John Cabot. Not because he thought Columbus had picked up all the marbles. Rather, because he didn't believe Columbus had found the Indies. His "Indians" weren't clothed in silks and jewels; they were "as naked as when their mothers bore them."

Like Columbus, Cabot had gathered all the information he could in Lisbon, that beehive of nautical lore. He may have suspected that what Columbus claimed for Spain was only that chain of islands that had appeared on various maps ever since 1424. Antillia's sands were said to be one third gold.*

*Though Columbus boldly labeled his plan "Enterprise of the Indies," Spanish records make no mention of the Indies or Asia. They refer instead to "certain islands in the sea of whose existence Columbus knew." He was to find them and take possession of them for Spain.

But Antillia wasn't the Indies. Somewhere beyond those islands, Asia lay waiting . . . waiting for Giovanni Caboto to reach and claim it.

It was probably while Columbus was sailing home—or earlier, or shortly after—that a ship out of Bristol at last found land to the west. Found North America.

This astonishing pronouncement contradicts what we were taught and demands explanation.

The evidence is an interesting old letter not resurrected until 1956. It was dredged from a mass of 33 *million* documents in the national archives of Spain at Simancas, where private as well as state papers are preserved. Though the date of the letter, 1497, puts us a bit ahead of our story, the event itself should be considered against its own background in time.

The letter is addressed to the "Almirante Mayor," likely Columbus, whose title by then was Admiral of the Ocean Sea. It was written by an Englishman, John Day, just after the Cabot discovery of 1497. Day wrote that the land Cabot discovered was "assumed and believed to be the mainland that the men from Bristol found" some years earlier.

Since the reappearance of this letter, many historians believe that English navigators whose names are forgotten reached the North American mainland no later than 1494. This opinion seems to be gaining ground. In due time it will find its way into textbooks.

What the men from Bristol found was probably Newfoundland. Clearly it wasn't golden Cathay. Nor was it laden with spices. Yet off its shores the ocean teemed with cod. Nowhere else in the world was there such an enormous abundance of fish as off the Grand Banks of Newfoundland. Now England had her own fisheries. Keeping the fishing grounds secret seemed at the time a good idea.

Whether John Cabot stood on the Bristol quay and watched the ship nose into port with a cargo of reeking cod instead of spices nobody knows. He might have been aboard with the cargo; or he might not yet have arrived in England. Either way, he knew or soon learned what the letter implies: that the men from Bristol realized they had found mainland. As he knew they would.

Cod. A lesser man might have been devastated, but Cabot only did some rethinking. Whether in private moments he called it Brasylle, Markland, Vinland, or still another name, he must have guessed that that rough northern land was not the Cathay he dreamed of, not the land whose rulers wore pearls and gold. And yet there was only one landmass. (This belief persisted; after all, Columbus himself had identified the New World as part of the Old.) Surely, then, a mainland to the west of Europe had to be Asia? And this not-so-distant mainland across from Ireland had to be an east-reaching arm of northern Asia? Maybe even Cathay's wild northern reaches? Why couldn't he follow its coast southwest until it led him to the riches of Cathay?

In 1496 he presented his plan to King Henry VII of England.

The king must have listened with mixed emotions. Not many years earlier he had turned down Columbus' plea to finance *his* expedition. The proposition, put to King Henry by Christopher's brother Bartholomew, had seemed at the time amusing—as well as outrageously expensive. The time for tears came later, when King Henry heard how Columbus, scarlet clad, splashed ashore on an Asian island, kissed the ground, planted the royal standard, and took possession of the land for Spain. Perhaps now, when John Cabot stood before him, King Henry reasoned that if Columbus had indeed found the forefront of the Indies, this fellow Cabot might yet find Cathay. He must carry along a royal standard.

King Henry issued letters patent authorizing John Cabot and his sons "to sail to the east, west, or north, with five ships carrying the English flag, to seek and discover all the islands, countries, regions, or provinces of the heathens in whatever part of the world." King Henry was to have one fifth of the profits.

It was May 2, 1497, when John Cabot and a crew of eighteen sailed from Bristol aboard a ship named the *Matthew.* He passed the southern coast of Ireland, held north for "some days," then west for thirty-five days across the North Atlantic. There was no steady trade wind on his stern such as pushed Columbus along farther south. On June 24, 1497, Cabot reached land, probably touching at Cape Breton north of Nova Scotia or at Newfoundland.

He unfurled the banners of England and Venice and solemnly took possession of the country.

A letter written that year states that Cabot spent the next month coasting along the land and covered almost a thousand miles—enough to convince him he had indeed found the mainland of Asia. He saw no people, but notched trees and snares for game suggested that people were not far away. Leaving, he came upon great schools of cod. The crew lowered baskets into the water and hoisted them brimming. Speeded homeward by westerly winds, he made the return voyage in fifteen days.

By August 6 Cabot was back in Bristol. From there he hastened to court and reported that he had reached the coast of Cathay "in the territory of the Grand Khan." He could not, however, find the Grand Khan himself and deliver to him King Henry's letter of introduction. Small matter. Even if Cabot had reached China, there had been no Grand Khan for more than a century, ever since the Ming dynasty swept the Mongols from power.

An observer in London noted that "honors are heaped upon Cabot, he is called Grand Admiral, he is dressed in silk, and the English run after him like madmen."

King Henry was less impressed. He awarded Cabot the sum of £10 "to have a good time with."

As it turned out, the English people had, after all, something to cheer about. John Cabot never reached China, but many years later, after Portuguese power had waned and the English had defeated the Spanish Armada, England spoke out. She claimed North America, basing her claim on that moment John Cabot planted the royal standard.

The news of 1497 never reached the dwindling group of Norsemen who still lived on in Greenland. Maybe it's just as well nobody told them. They might have found it confusing: John Cabot discovering Greater Vinland, recognizing it as China, and claiming it for England. They never saw another merchant ship gliding up Eriksfjord, bringing the latest styles and the news of Europe, even bringing, they hoped, a priest to replace the last priest, who died in 1412. They never saw another European.

The bold were steering across farther south—toward the gold of the Indies. The Greenlanders' five-hundred-year struggle to maintain their distant outpost of civilization was almost over.

Yet Norse descendants apparently lived on in America, some not very far from where John Cabot planted the English standard. The earliest English explorers said of the Newfoundland natives, "The colour of their hair was divers, some blacke, some browne, and some yellow."

In 1534 the French navigator Jacques Cartier sailed

through the Strait of Belle Isle and discovered warmer, more fertile regions. He was the first post-Columbian explorer to reach Prince Edward Island, New Brunswick, Chaleur Bay, and the Gaspé Peninsula. We know him as the discoverer of the St. Lawrence River. Back home, he reported seeing a region where the natives were "as white as the people of France."

How do we account for such people in a region presumably never before explored? Do we charge flatly that Cartier saw no such thing? Do we suspect the disputed Portuguese-Scandinavian expedition of fraternizing with the Quii people? Or do we see in those white natives some former Greenlanders who fled to America a century earlier when pirates were ravaging Greenland?

As the world moved into the sixteenth century, Greenland itself seemed to vanish in northern mists. A long time later, a minister in Norway named Hans Egede read about the Norse Greenlanders and was overwhelmed by the urge to go there and convert them to Christianity. In 1721 he landed on the west coast of Greenland and started looking. To his dismay he found no Norsemen—only Eskimos. All of Greenland belonged to the Eskimos.

The written records, too, had vanished. Perhaps the people of the Eastern Settlement had moved away and carried their records with them. Perhaps the records burned when pirates burned the churches. Or perhaps, when the last surviving Norseman in Greenland had died, Eskimos found the parchments and, lacking knowledge of the written word, set the records afire to warm their hands.

The Norsemen's five hundred years in Greenland had ended.

As we close the book on the Vikings, we wonder how they accomplished as much as they did, so few with so little—

without compass, quadrant, or astrolabe, without musket or rifle. Their courage was great, but they lived too soon. They lived before Europe was ready to find a new world.

The full story can never be told, never wholly reassembled from shards, from a stone lamp here or a spindle whorl there. Yet from such mute witnesses modern research is trying to reconstruct the past. Now and then it gets an assist when a crumbling letter is discovered in dusty archives.

Already enough has been learned that schoolchildren never again will be taught that only the American Indians came here before Columbus. Or, as a history textbook put it just twenty years ago, "Vikings touched on these shores briefly and sailed away." The story of early America is immensely richer than most of us dreamed.

Some of the bravest chapters of American history have been open only a little while for all to read. And some are still closed, awaiting the touch of curious fingers.

For Further Reading

The reader interested in pursuing this subject would do well to read Gwyn Jones's *The Norse Atlantic Saga* (Oxford, 1964). Professor Jones, one of the finest scholars in this field, leavens his knowledge with Welsh wit as he tells how Norsemen, hungering for land that was "habitable and trespassable," moved westward across the Atlantic to Iceland, to Greenland, and finally to the American continent. The second half of the book provides English translations of the Greenlanders' Saga, Erik's Saga, *Íslendingabók* and *Landnámabók*.

Other books too include full translations of the two Vinland sagas. Among them, my long-time favorite is G. M. Gathorne-Hardy's *The Norse Discoverers of America: The Wineland Sagas Translated and Discussed* (Oxford, Clarendon Press, 1921). Gathorne-Hardy was one of the first to suggest that the Greenlanders' Saga records the Greenland tradition, and Erik the Red's Saga records the Icelandic.

Another is Arthur Middleton Reeves's *The Finding of Wineland the Good* (London, Frowde, 1895), reprinted in 1967 (Burt Franklin), a unique work in that it reproduces both manuscripts in facsimile. Opposite each handwritten, time-mottled page, every line of the Old Norse is transcribed in standard type, also in Old Norse. Reeves's English translations sound somewhat archaic now, but his footnotes explaining certain words, though they seem too pedantic to some, will interest those who want to go into this subject with care. An introductory section of the book examines references to Vinland in other medieval sources.

Very different is Einar Haugen's *Voyages to Vinland* (Knopf, 1942). His translations are informal, almost slangy, but reliable.

A slim paperback that consists largely of the translations, introduced by 37 pages of perceptive comments, is *The Vinland Sagas: The Norse Discovery of America,* by Magnus Magnusson and Hermann Pálsson (Penguin Books, 1965; reprinted in hardcover by New York University Press in 1966).

The student who wants to learn the history of the Vikings other than their American endeavors will find it in Gwyn Jones's *A History of the Vikings* (Oxford, 1968), which traces the Scandinavians from their legendary beginnings through the triumphs of Canute the Great, Danish king of England, to their final defeat in England in 1066. This book is more difficult than Jones's *Norse Atlantic Saga.*

Another good one on the same subject is T. D. Kendrick's *A History of the Vikings* (Scribner, 1930; Barnes & Noble, 1968). Kendrick, who was in the British Museum's Department of British and Medieval Antiquities, traces the birth of the Viking nations and follows Vikings abroad to the east as well as the west.

A paperback on the history of the Vikings is Johannes Brøndsted's *The Vikings* (Penguin Books, 1960). After devoting five chapters to history, Brøndsted moves on to a discussion of Viking weapons, dress, ships, runic inscriptions, art, way of life, religious beliefs, and poetry. Brøndsted was highly esteemed as the director of the National Museum in Copenhagen.

Easier reading and covering much the same range as Brøndsted is Jacqueline Simpson's *Everyday Life in the Viking Age* (Putnam, 1967). Its 121 small black-and-white illustrations capture the spirit of the age.

Both Brøndsted and Simpson discuss Viking ships, but the reader whose curiosity is not slaked by a chapter can learn more by reading William Hovgaard's *Voyages of the Norsemen to Amer-*

ica (American Scandinavian Foundation, 1914). Hovgaard had wide knowledge of the Vikings, their Vinland voyages, and especially their ships: He was professor of Naval Design and Construction at the Massachusetts Institute of Technology.

A book devoted solely to the ships is *The Viking Ships, Their Ancestry and Evolution,* by A. W. Brøgger and Haakon Shetelig (Oslo, Dreyer, 1951). When they wrote this, no *knorr* had ever been recovered. The plebeian *knerrir* were not granted burial like the grander Norse ships; a *knorr* that became unseaworthy was usually plundered for nails and planks. So it was a momentous day when five Viking ships from around the year 1000 were discovered on the muddy bottom of Roskilde Fjord, Denmark, where they had been sunk to block the channel against invaders. As divers brought up the pieces, archaeologists realized that here was at least one *knorr*, possibly two. These five ships are described in an article, "The Skuldelev Ships," by Olaf Olsen and Ole Crumlin-Pedersen in *Acta Archaeologica*, Vol. XXXVIII (1967), pp. 73–174. Now reconstructed, these ships are preserved in the Roskilde ship museum.

As vital to Norse seafarers as their ships was the ability to find their way across oceans. A particularly helpful article on how the Vikings navigated is G. J. Marcus' "The Navigation of the Norsemen" in *Mariner's Mirror*, Vol. XXXIX, No. 2 (May 1953), pp. 112–31. Another source is Farley Mowat's *Westviking: The Ancient Norse in Greenland and North America* (Little, Brown, 1965); Appendix F, pp. 351–63, is entitled "Norse Navigation." (There's also an appendix on Norse seagoing ships.) Mowat's brash and sometimes heretical book presents a reconstruction of the westward voyages, based on the sagas plus what *he* would have done if faced with the same decisions. A resident of Newfoundland when he wrote this, Mowat knew firsthand the terrain he describes and had long experience with ships and the sea.

The student whose appetite for literature of exploration has been whetted might want to go on to Samuel Eliot Morison's *The European Discovery of America: The Northern Voyages* (Oxford,

1971). The master biographer of Columbus devotes a single chapter to the Norsemen and Vinland. It makes great reading, but proceed with caution: It contains some errors, set down with Morison's customary assurance. Nevertheless, this thick volume, at once lively and scholarly, is an excellent introduction to explorations in the North Atlantic from the wanderings of St. Brendan, the seagoing Irish abbot, to the founding of the Virginia colonies, made more vivid by excellent illustrations.

If this awakens a thirst for more, try John Fiske's three-volume work *The Discovery of America* (Houghton, Mifflin, 1892). These are by no means dusty tomes. Here is another scholar who writes with the same verve, the same absence of academic tedium, as Morison.

Turning now from expansion to specialization, to reading in depth in one area, let's start with Greenland. To visualize the locales described in the sagas, from the bleak east coast to Erik the Red's Brattahlid to Lysufjord and Norðrsetur, try Helge Ingstad's *Land under the Pole Star* (St. Martin's Press, 1966). Then, to people these sites with Norsemen, turn to Poul Nørlund's *Viking Settlers in Greenland and Their Descendants during Five Hundred Years* (London, Cambridge University Press, 1936). As one of the archaeologists who uncovered these sites, Nørlund speaks with authority on such matters as their clothes and customs.

Moving south to L'Anse aux Meadows, Newfoundland, we can read about its discovery and excavation in *Westward to Vinland* (St. Martin's Press, 1969) by the discoverer himself, Helge Ingstad. Here again are numerous illustrations.

Moving still farther south, Frederick Pohl offers his evidence for Vinland in New England in *The Lost Discovery* (Norton, 1952) and *The Viking Settlements of North America* (Potter, 1972). Some may want to linger in New England to read for themselves and evaluate cryptographer Alf Mongé's analysis of what he firmly believes to be runic messages found on certain stones there. The book to consult is *Norse Medieval Cryptography in Runic Carvings* by Alf Mongé and O. G. Landsverk (Norseman Press, 1967).

Landsverk carries this further in his *Runic Records of the Norsemen in America* (Twayne, 1974). In the former book Mongé also sets forth his analysis of the Kensington Stone, so we move on to Minnesota.

The case for Minnesota has as its major protagonist Hjalmar R. Holand, who wrote several books on the Norse in that state but did not live to see Alf Mongé's corroboration. Those who would like to assess Holand's evidence should start with his *Westward from Vinland* (Duell, Sloan & Pearce, 1940). It was reprinted a generation later under its earlier subtitle, *Norse Discoveries and Explorations in America, 982–1362* (Dover, 1969).

Finally, the curious-minded who want to know what happened *after* may wish to read James Robert Enterline's *Viking America: The Norse Crossings and Their Legacy* (Doubleday, 1972). Enterline's primary concern is what went on in the "gap" between the sagas and Columbus' discovery. This book opens the mind to new conceptions. It's provocative and controversial.

In fact, much of what has been published about the Norse in America is controversial, from A.D. 985 on (a date sometimes given as A.D. 986, on less convincing evidence, I believe). In suggesting these further readings, I have tried to give representation to variant points of view.

These are only a few of the books available, and the articles number many more; the best articles are in scholarly journals. It is my hope that some who have just finished reading this book will feel the urge to explore more widely into America's greatest mystery and perhaps, in time, will even discover additional clues to America's tantalizing past.

Index